'Introduction'

In 1989, during my study on subject 'Unorganized sectors and lack of social security', I visited numerous old age homes and contacted the aged men and women. Some said lack of financial support, some said had no children, some only had daughters, they didn't want to burden them, some accounted homelessness, but many accused torture and disparagement by daughters in law, coerced them to leave home.

On asking why sons cannot be blamed? Their straight answer was "they knew their sons since the birth. The son transmutes attitude only under wife's influence." An aged woman admitted by saying "It's the spark once caught when newlywed wife entered in our home. My mistreatment over time transformed the spark into wild fire. Today is her day to avenge but she too has the day what I face today." Another aged man said "the economic crisis isn't only the reason to kick the parents out. It's the will that counts. Will she do the same to her mother and father?" The mistreated elders finally resort to old age shelters or wander in the streets.

Yet, in many houses I observe affection still exist. The cordial relationship still holds on. My inquisitiveness actuated me to ask many such families. Some said daughter in law was known to them since the childhood. Some said she is really nice, understands us. Some said we share sad or joy together. There I understood is how both accept each other. They never crossed each other's boundary.

Domestic violence in any configuration is triggered by accumulation of small-small untoward incidences, bursts one day. You can resolve easily by sharing and communicating with each other. Things you don't like, say at face, but softly without hurting ego, perhaps later, when the fire is extinguished. Mend it; no one is perfect all need guidelines for modification.

The girl comes to your home isn't familiar with your system. It's very new for her. You might have observed her shame, hesitation and fear when she first entered your house. Gestures the system she had in her own home was totally different. Thither she was a daughter, and here in your home, she is a daughter in law. The crisis arises where you only expect her to adjust, but you don't relax your mold so she fits in easily. She expects love and warmth so she forgets the pain of leaving own home.

In my own house, I experienced a similar situation with my mother and my wife. Both were like a snake and mongoose. Both attempted to extrude each other from home. Many a times, I felt myself as grain getting crushed between two grinding stones. However, an acquaintance of mine's guidance helped me; I preferred to remain impartial for both than partial to one. That managed my home, though they still have a hostile relationship yet both are with me in own home. Finally, I came to conclusion that mother in law's fear of losing grip over home and daughter in law's wish for a family of her own choice together clues to burst into spark. The spark over time shapes into furious flame. There are a number of reasons of failing relationships; all are as a result of mismatching attitude. The reason may be the wife came from a different atmosphere and mother's denial to reshape ambiance so the newcomer adjusts easily into it.

An aged woman of 80 was found wandering in Guruvayur temple premises. On asking she said her son and the daughter in law had abandoned her. As a result of memory loss could not grasp the location of her son's house. In such case if a missing person's neighbor or distant relation had been tempted reward for reporting the missing, recoverable from the offenders, could have worked out the situation to claim maintenance. The temple authority said "most dumped elderly are women. Roughly 15 destitute ends up in the lap of Lord Krishna as free food are served at noon and the evening." Such incidences do happen off and on in many cities and semi urban centers. The senior citizen protection Act 2007 should see all facets to protect to elderly.

A similar case of an aged woman in good faith had transferred her property in son's name. But did not realize the son would conspire and abandon her in the Cochin Airport before going away abroad. The miserable woman had nowhere to go waited and waited until police arrived. When in suspicion a policeman asked, she showed the ticket without visa. The police realized the conspiracy of the son and his wife. Lastly, she told the whole story to the police and settled down in an old age home.

We have several brutal examples prove the cultural failure. If she had written a 'will' instead of outright gifting the property, the situation would have been different. I suggest, the senior citizen protection Act 2007, should have provision of only 'will' by elderly. No sale or transfer authorized legally in case documented in old age over 70 in case of males (widowers) and 65 in case of females (widows). Among such victims majority are aged women, this step would save them from destitute state.

In one incidence the father widower had a double storey house in Raja Garden, Delhi. He had four sons living in the same household. The father was murdered brutally because he loved his youngest son. Now is very common to read such news in the papers. The world is transforming from social values to material values. Accordingly, we should be prepared for untoward incidences. In Delhi most aged are registered by local police stations, but follow up is negligible.

- Senior citizens should also have a clear cut mind that who takes care is the kin.

- Also should keep in mind all glittering shine is not genuine; it may be a fraud too.

- The aged are the easiest victims in this modern world. Own children can plot a murder to grab the valuables. Don't blind your eyes, report to nearby police even slightest doubt or suspicious activity you find from own kin's or outsiders.

- Having a locker in Police station to preserve property documents and valuable assets of aged above 70 in case of male, and 65 incase of woman widow is added security to senior citizens.

- Only the senior citizen owner of the documents may be allowed to consider transacting that too in the supervision of not less than the Assistant commissioner of police.

I have a friend of age 78, name 'Patbanabhan'. After his retirement from Indian Railways gets the pension, but has no own house. Moans, all his life what earned had spent on raising two children and treating wife's cancer. Today, both the children don't want him. Lives alone in a rented house eat up half of his earning as rent. He married twice, but both had passed away of cancer. Many times in sobbing voice he sounds out the loneliness tortures him at this old age. He states "old age is already cruel, but when don't get support from own blood hurts. They are my blood can't even curse them. Where did I fail raising them?" In that respect, there are several people and their miserable stories I have enciphered in this volume.

In each household there are issues and problems of new and old generation. The unfillable gap exists yet with the adjustments by both new and old generation together design home scenic. Elders are embellishments of a house as many dwelling houses are decorated with old antique. Their presence is enough to create an ambiance to inspire.

The only wish of many aged "We want nothing; take all from us whatever we have. But share some time and listen to what we have. We don't live to hurt you, but need a bit of care and a feel of recourse. We also lived through the age you have. We too were tied and gave birth to kids like you. Mother and Father had their position; we could never dare challenge in our times. They had respect and we had respect. Please don't neglect us; we make mistakes, forgive us as you do with your kids"

There are so many issues of domestic crisis, but the solution is one word 'contentment', thwarts all strategic tools of the fiend. When you have this in your mind, you have everything.

The base cause of all unpleasant happenings in or outside home, we are getting greedy day by day in this luxuriously economic world. Money, wealth and money power have encroached our minds. The social thinking is transforming to accumulation of wealth without giving place to the kinship. We aren't happy and content with what we receive. The greed has no limit, extends before you accomplish one. Ego arises from inferiority complex. Ire is a mark of helplessness. Concern arises from the guilt and lack one has. Content people are complete and find exigency within their range. They live in philosophy don't look for love hither and thither when you have one at home. Each individual is beautiful, some have outer beauty and some hold inside. Accept as is and embellish to feel the gaiety.

Nothing is yours except the 'contentment' while giving love the aura of your spirit enhances. You leave everything behind when you depart this earth except the gain from karma and love you gave. Love is monumental, always remembered even after your death.

Children may make many mistakes owing to lack of experience, but 'forgiveness' tool is in your hand, use it so they kneel before you. The pain behind 'forgiving' will wriggle and coerce them to say sorry. You are matured, but the children still have to attain maturity to reach close to your wisdom. They are like infants step forward to learn walking or ascend. During their practice several times they fall and fail without realizing mother or father behind them to support. Elders have still the same role, let them fail, let them fall, but make them realize you are behind them in support.

You should examine carefully the seed before sowing. Nurture it carefully so doesn't spoil. The quality of fruit you grow is an outcome of your efforts and devotion involved.

When kids grow enough to wear shoes of your size, they are no more kids. Accepting daddy or mummy's control hurts their freedom and choice. However, if they know you are behind them in support is a boon for them, they feel you are the best friend can rely on.

Each one has a problem in this world as a result of undue craving. Sometimes things don't come to your expectation stresses you, results exertion. Sometimes your craving is beyond your competence agitates you, incur efforts assertively to achieve is also a form of disruptisfaction, when fail frustrates you. Therefore, the positivity is to do your best and if fail accept with cheer. Halt for some time and attempt again and once more calmly. Failure is not you lost all, rather, is a

4

lesson to correct deficiency before climbing next step of the ladder. Content with what you have is the philosophy of life for happiness.

Even when you watch your hand, the fingers aren't of the same size, yet, are together in one hand contributing own roles. One more tip, when you point your finger at others, you should also watch the three fingers you fold are pointing you. Thus, change is needed in you too.

The entire awkward situation arises as an outcome of upbringing in an environment that influences negativity/ positivity in one's conduct. Negative influence stimulates our negativity to rise. However, when the mind and emotional state is strongly positive, no outside negative force can act upon. Fear, greed, scruple, selfishness, ecstatic desire and impishness are evil's strategic tools to desecrate peaceful home life. Beware of its intention, its endeavor to seduce you by ephemeral ecstatic avarice.

Trust is the foundation of all good relationships. A relationship is like love marsh, has the ability to drown in. Both are responsible to attract each other to retain pleasing home ambience, so lasts even when away from domicile. When both live together each has a liability to caress the other. *Some persons aren't content with what they own; wander hither and thither to look for happiness without realizing the happiness comes up from within. Search inside self, you will find what you need. Love you find when you know love. Wandering for love is no love; it only shoves you towards skepticism and disloyalty.* Also eludes failures in handling responsibilities. *Enduring sufferings makes you stronger and more potent. Be cool and don't be scared, learn to face it, sufferings will fail one day.* Ability to defeat the negativity is the competence.

Ages back in South Asian countries, the system of joint family had prevailed. The seniors were the most respectful. In all decision making systems they were not only involved, but their guidelines too were considered. Elders looked daughter and daughter in law in same eye. Each daughter in law and mother in law had tendency to care each other. Those days are past now in this developed modern world.

I narrate a story of baya weaving bird of **'Nest and Home':**

Once I watched in the tree,
Over the shore of a lake;
Baya weaver, weaving nest;
Once it wove,
Sat back in open branch;
Danced and fluttered wings,
Gestured keen by flirting girls;
See the nest, I made it's for you;

She comes, examines nest,
Hither, thither around the nest;
Your dance is good, you are good,
Your nest is very good,
But not made for me;
Goes back to other dancing males;
The male reweaves his nest,
Waits on the branch,
Dances, flutters his wings,
Attracting girls, says,
I weave a nest,
Touches your heart;
She inspects around the nest,
Enters, makes the alteration;
Modifies to suit her ambiance,
Adorns the nest for future kids;
Comes to him makes some love;
When ready, she lays her egg,
Sits over hatches eggs,
Man goes out, brings some food;
It's a man, makes a nest,
Women comes makes nest a home;
With no woman there is no home;
Children add up spice for spicy home;
Mother in law should spare a space,
So daughter in law builds her home;
Obstacle to it is a conflict,
Natural instinct a woman has,
Won't like anyone taking her space;

The characters and the theme in the story may be artificial, but based on real life experiences of many. The emotional and physical pains they endure touch our spirit. Where will we end up don't know yet. We will be no different from animals, drive out the aged from group to confront miserable lonely life. Is this the society we have ahead? The stories in this book may hurt feelings of some. But rest assures we too will be victims of modern attitude of modern world.

Live and let live

Dry leaves

As early as 6 in the morning! The rising sun was radiating earth; breeze strewing its cool aroma soothing life on land. Twittering birds on top of the trees were vibrating environment with gorgeous musical sound. Blossom petals were wet with dew gesturing a new fresh day. People were busy walking, running and doing yoga so were fit for the rest the day. The garden was packed with young, old and kids seeking freshness.

Autumn golden dry leaves scattered all over reminder of nothing is immortal in this world. You retreat to give space to young. Your deeds are over, but you have experiences, you need to share with tender young. Your experiences and their deeds together contribute to worldly life, because history is the foundation of the future. It is the universal theory for moving the worldly affairs.

Darshan, Prem and Saleem, all were age group of 62-65, among others, on a dawn walk in the Lodi Garden Park. Away from polluted city enjoying company and chatting past experiences. Nature too propitiated open heartedly through its bright sunshine and cool breeze, enjoying smiling faces of passerby.

They were closest friends for over two decades, missed never a day without gossip and boring Saleem's poems.

While walking Darshan saw dry leaf dropping from the tree, flowing in the air getting away from easy catch. He raced a few steps to hold in hand.

In exhilaration Darshan said "'wow' finally found the dried leaf in my hand"

"A retired leaf relieved from active role. The poor, dry leaf is like us now!" Prem commented

Dazed by Prem's comment Darshan said "'Ooh right', all life forms is forced to resign one day when is weak to execute"

Saleem took a dry leaf in his hand to sniff and pestle "neither aroma nor any juice, yet welcomed by mother earth."

"Yes, it knows the worth of this dry leaf as is part of it" Prem said

Saleem in deep thoughts, moving his lips quietly, grumbling self "a cruel natural world, it can't stand the sweetness when we ripe."

"Hey! What are you whispering, is there again a clash in your home?" Darshan asked

"No...Not that, I am already immune to Son and his wife's shameless behavior. I was whispering different. Old age signals, it's time to depart, but we are still in

7

queue, wait until turn comes. Day by day and inch by inch body and mind wither to prevent movements as no more deeds needed to accomplish. Does not mean we are a wasteland. Though the physical construction is no more needed, yet is meant for the following stages of deeds to bear. We divvy up all accumulated earnings during the lifetime span, with others to carry their deeds" Saleem said in misery voice "Don't know what God desires from us."

They walked for about two hours; their hearts pulsated fast as a result of intense breathing, and sat on a bench to relax near yoga session led by a yogi who was also a social worker. Darshan took a bottle of water and waited for some time for comfort before drinking he shared with others. Together started watching yoga, and commented on each posture of exercise and its advantages.

Saleem asked "did you ever go to yoga classes?"

"Never" both in one voice said

Saleem, looking stout at Prem smiled and said "Yoga has an advantage of activating aura and energizing organs. Yoga cools your body, freshens your mind. People attend yoga are happier than normal people."

Prem understood where he was and said "I may be wrong, without sound sleep for the body to function freely, yoga never achieves. Stress less life, drinking enough water and little regular walk is added advantage to body healing. Happiness releases endorphins, dopamine, serotonin and oxytocin chemicals in the brain to glow body and face."

Darshan wasn't satisfied and he asserted "In this materialistic world, drinking water and air is polluted, food is poisoned and basics are adulterated. In such state, how can you expect any meditation or yoga to give results?"

"We are lucky to survive the cruel world, but worried for our children and grandchildren. How will they endure painful diseases by polluted world?" Saleem expressed his concern

The atmosphere had bewildered them, looked at each other's face in a deep gasp.

"World needs a change for truthful life where human life is more valuable than wealth" Saleem quoted. However, he wanted to change the mood of friends to normal, so came with a new poem...

Want change!

Don't ever dare
think of changing world,
Change the way thou see
this world,

Change the way thou think
this world;
change thy thoughts,
Not by fashion dress,
Nor by expensive car,
Change by novel thoughts;
Change freshens your life,
World will look fresh to you
You are new so the world is new;

"Yes, sure, if each individual thinks this way, the world would be pretty habitable" Darshan said

"I guess so, the materialistic life has totally corrupted human behavior" Prem said

"Yes, you are right, children are so busy day and night, unable to spare time for own parents and children." Darshan reclined his head in grief while saying

Saleem assented, said "Yee... *Tender leaf doesn't realize dry leaf is its future.* That's life, my friend." He thought of a verse form "now listen to my poem"

We are dry leaves...
Once were fresh;
Green lush and alluring,
Same like you;
Sought fresh breeze,
Discharged rancid breath,
We were once,
Source of growth,
But now we are aged
No more use of tree,
Don't step on us,
Don't crush by foot,
Gives us pain,
Hurts our heart,
Pierces our soul,
We are dry leaves...
We once were fresh...
But it's now autumn
we are back to earth
World discards aged,
But don't know,
we were also part of growth;

Live and let live

Yoga teacher 'Shankar' aged 70, listened three friends' conversation. After finishing his yoga class, he decided to join them. Before joining, he made up in his mind "I have to transform their negativity."

Came forth holding both palms together over chest greeted "Namaste, may I join you?"

'Namaste' is the Sanskrit word derived from *'Nama' – Bow, 'Ast' – I, 'Te' – You. 'I bow to you'* prevalent since Vedic Age. Both palms held together close to the chest gestures the gratitude and veneration.

"Yes, why not" Prem said

"Our pleasure" Saleem thankfully said

Shankar introduced himself and smiled before speaking "I have come to clear your doubts over isolated aging life"

Prem, Darshan and Saleem curiously waited the words from Shankar's mouth.

Shankar explained "*Even when you watch your hand, the fingers aren't of the same size, yet, are together in one hand contributing own roles. One more tip, when you point your finger at others, you should also watch the three fingers you fold are pointing you. Therefore, change is needed in you too.*"

The presence of yoga teacher fascinated others too to join, including young married and aged. It was good for Shankar to understand the depth of crisis with valuable opinions of young and aged both.

"*In each household there are issues and problems of new and old generation. The unfillable gap exists yet with the adjustments by both new and old generations, design together home scenic. Elders are embellishments of a home as many homes are adorned with old antiques. Their presence is enough to create an atmosphere to inspire*" Shankar stressed while speaking

"We are well wishers can't watch our children straggling. They are our kids!" Saleem said

The discussion was getting hot as many supporters and non-supporters assembled. Felt the blaze, some finally found a platform to quench the burning pain piled up inside for several years. People were looking each other who was first to express.

'War of women and son gets crushed'

A matured man evinced courage and stood up to say "What I saw in many houses reveals that modern generation is losing interest in joint family structure and hate elder's control. Women now feel freer than ever before, so now they are ahead to exercise. Nuclear family may be as a result of women exercising freedom."

The woman seemed his wife couldn't stand words from him, yelled "my foot! It's all because of a jealous mother in law, your mother. Why doesn't she behave the same way with her daughter as she behaves with me? What freedom you are talking? We are also as human as you. Why don't you accept the truth? Women are now literate and confident. We have begun realizing the role of women in this world. We can live by ourselves without the support of men."

Her husband was blushed shamefaced reclined his head. He did not expect her anguish explosion in public which she had carried inside for long without letting him know. She held his hand scrubbed to soothe and said calmly "I did not mean to hurt you"

"You should have discussed with me," he whispered in her ear

"How could I when you were totally inclined to your parents," she said

"You have embarrassed me in public," he replied nipping her arm

The attention of all diverted towards them consoling "its life, none is perfect, and mistakes are for solutions, it's you to overcome."

She looked at him and maintained silence to avoid fallacy. "Let's go," she said

"No… The discussion is good, we should stay. May be, we may find some good points for transformation"

Another young married adult female from the audience came forth to explain her dissonance and said "I don't hate my mother in law or her hubby. I go wild when she rags me and that man keeps watching without saying a word to her. No day goes without fight, complaints, blames and screams from her the moment I enter the house. After office work I have to do cooking at home and at night in bed. I am a human how long I can survive such brutality. I don't know why she is so jealous and panic of my presence at home. They are testing my patience. One day I will revolt and shout back, will spark the ferocity. *Elders are to support and not control.*"

Some other woman from the lot accorded with her and said "for me the marriage was love, but reversed all my aspirations when I entered new home, same situation I had faced. My father in law was always supportive. Always interfered, nevertheless, failed to resolve the situation. Eventually, when things went out of control he asked us to leave home and set up own. Straight off we shifted and now we are happy, have cordial relation with the mother and father in law. I consider her as my own mother and will forever be there for both of them"

Shankar felt the feelings of surrounding audience and said "*When kids grow enough to wear shoes of your size, they are no more kids. Accepting daddy or mummy's control hurts their freedom and choice.* Treat them as the closest friends. And then see, with no reluctance they enjoy your companionship. They feel bliss, sharing day to day occurrences and seek counseling. Fit in their frame as they did in their childhood, listen to them. Guide them as a good friend; they will enjoy your lively feelings. It's the best way to narrow the gap between you and the kids. Don't you believe it? Test it, you will believe for sure."

"But we have no grievances with our sons, we have no issues. Our issue is with his woman. She does not treat us as humans" Saleem complained

"Now you please note my point. *The girl comes to your home isn't familiar with your system. It's very new for her. You might have observed her shame, hesitation and fear when she first entered your home. Gestures the system she had in her own home was totally different. There she was a daughter, and here in your home, she is a daughter in law. You only expect her to adjust, but you don't relax your mold so she fits in. She expects love and warmth so she forgets the pain of leaving own home.*" Shankar explained

Young and middle aged married women felt relieved and one said "the truth has come out finally."

One young man roughly of 30 years asserted the complaint of his wife sitting beside him "my wife only listen to her mothers' discourse and behaves accordingly. I don't live with mother or father to mother in law touch. But my wife's inclination drives me to divorce her. Her mother is more poisonous than a mother in law. No more I can stand my wife's behavior; sometimes I feel she is insane"

The wife immediately stood up saying "my mother guides me to protect me from any untoward"

"Thank you, finally you have accepted that your mother is behind all. Now we cannot live together anymore" the boy said and went away

The wife too stood and went along with him saying "next time I will prohibit her indulging in our matter"

"Sorry, it is enough now I cannot endure anymore" the boy said lamenting and whispered "both mothers in laws are poison to newlywed life. I will look for better match."

"*You should examine carefully the seed before sowing. Nurture it carefully so doesn't spoil. The quality of fruit you get is an outcome of your endeavors and devotion involved.*" Shankar elucidated

Darshan presented his counter opinion "*But, sometimes dedication, nurturing too fail when they come in contact with wretched atmosphere. Parents fail to watch their kids' activities and association as a result of lack of time. Inattentiveness causes young's link with negativity, in the end we repent. Thus sages have guided us to pay attention right from the beginning. Give them love and touch they want so they are free to move with you. Make them understand good and bad about being spoilt."*

"Yes, this is a point; it's all about how your upbringing is! A Major portion of behavioral development is by parents. When they miss, things begin failing. Yes, it's true." Shankar commented accepting Darshan's words.

"Nothing is yours except the 'contentment' while giving love the aura of your spirit enhances. You leave everything behind when you depart this earth except the gain from karma and love you gave. Love is monumental, always remembered even after the death. Children may make many mistakes owing to lack of experience, but 'forgiveness' the tool is in your hand, use it so they kneel before you. The pain behind 'forgiving' will wriggle and coerce them to say sorry. You are matured, but the children still have to attain maturity as you." Shankar said

Shankar himself got emotional while saying as he too had experienced haunting situations. Many a days he did not turn up home so could escape horrid situation of facing mother and wife. Whenever he entered home both were ready to serve complaints. None were ready to accommodate."

Subsequently engaging a mysterious breath, gave out his silence and expressed painful feelings "Also, I advice daughter in laws too, not to mix up past home with a new dwelling house so your future home is amicable where you, your hubby and your kids live without past grudge."

One married man showed up to say "My mother is my mother Goddess for me, carried for nine months and nurtured me during my needs. I look, talk, walk, and do all because of father and mother. I need their blessings for all my life. I want my mom and pop both with me as they were the only hope in my infancy. They loved my first walk, they enjoyed my first talk and they supported my advancement. I want them with me as long as they are alive, so I survive under their shadow. At the same time my wife is a companion. She motivates me, loves me, shares all ifs and buts with me and on top of all, she is the mother of my kids. I feel solaced and warmth when she hugs and kisses me. For me both are important, however, situations sometimes haunt me. I feel like getting crushed between two grinding stones. Both women don't realize the painful situation they are creating for me. Tell me who suffers the most in their ego and jealous clash"

Another person nodded while saying "Indian culture still survives in rural villages where elders have respect. I am from a rural village and married, have two kids. My wife is a postgraduate and runs a community school. Usually she is busy until eventide. In her absence my mother takes care of home and my kids. There is no division of work at all; both enter the kitchen and my father in the farm. If one is tired the other helps. If both are sick and tired, my father takes charge of taking care of both. I never have issues as you have in urban cities. In villages the wedding is a ritual ceremony of a tie between two villages or communities. If any issue surfaces, is a disgrace to the community. The entire village involves to solving before blows up. Indeed, there are several restrictions for both mother and daughter in law and each member of the family, which has to be strictly followed. The sages aren't fools to create social law and order systems."

"What do you mean? Women should be sent back behind the curtain" Chitra impolitely yelled

"No, I did not mean that, my wife too goes to work, that doesn't mean she shouldn't follow the social ideology. The absence of cultural values unnecessarily prompts domestic violence, rape, separation, Daughter in law and Mother in law conflicts, absence of mutual respect." He replied

A young Chitra agonized by his remarks retorted "my foot! Do you think women are slaves for use and throw? These impudent acts are of uncultured men spurred by family backgrounds. I am a free woman don't give damn to marriage."

Some other woman from the crowd shouted at him "shut up you stupid uncivilized village man, that was past when women were slaves. People like you, encourage injustice to women"

"Sorry, if I have injured your feelings," he bowed down and said.

Chitra was a bit embarrassed by his humbleness "No, you needn't say sorry. I am responsible for using harsh words. However, I have to clear my agony which still haunts my family. My sister was burnt alive 3 years ago for not meeting dowry demand." She held her handkerchief to wipe tears, looked at all in her red wet eyes.

Other women came forward to comfort her by embracing and kissing.

A girl Aabidah, human right campaigner said "there is no forgiveness for criminal greedy acts. Beautiful brides are burnt shamelessly for want of dowry. No stringent punishment in law yet, that sets an example to others. Such situations coerce women to disrespect and disintegrate from existing social structure."

Darshan went towards Chitra took her to his chest "don't weep, please, this morose us. Girls like you should gain courage to revolt and get justice for needy."

Shankar stooped, his head remembered past "we have heard the lively stories of these men and women. It's entirely because she doesn't feel at home as with her parents. Indeed, many houses are cursed by evil misfortunes. Married sons are victims of Mother and Daughter in law clashes. I too had experienced the same situation in the past. My mother wished to control my wife from the day she entered home. There was no day without a clash. My wife too, inflamed by her mother, persuaded me several times to break apart from home. I together with father objected and gave no option to both. Somehow our reluctance and my father's persistence to improve paid, situation transformed overtime when they realized both were and would be once daughter or mother in law. In their old age, they had to endure the situation and seek support of each other."

Saleem asked "why this happens? I don't know, these women fight and we become victims"

Simon, aged 70 the fourth friend of three, too, was present watching them carefully. His family was bold and frank. Had some problems initially with mom and wife as a result of confusion, but they adjusted easily.

He also had his views which he explained "Mother's sense, in most cases never accepts outside girl as her own daughter. In addition, the fear of losing sovereignty coerces her to demur. One more point, she is a mother first and her instinct wishes her son remains in her charge as before. Her aggressive behavior denotes the suspicion of losing a son from her. Thus, both remain cautious from crossing lines saves the family."

"It looks natural phenomenon avoiding competition to save headship. Happens with all species" A man from the crowd said

Some railed at him "we aren't animals"

"But behave like animals. Say for mother and daughter in law crisis and disregarding aged. Are these not animal behaviors?"

The crowd was silent without any remark as was the truth. But one said "If we have to show up ourselves as different from animals we have to behave like human"

It was already 9am. Birds had stopped their tweets and gestured it was time to go to work. People began the feel of Sun's glimmering heat. Some were to go to college, and some to office. Waited a chance to skip so could reach on time.

Shankar stood up holding both palms together and said "Namaskaar" to all "We are already late, let's go. Tomorrow come early at 5, we will discuss further."

A woman from the dispersing crowd "such discussions are important I feel relieved"

"Yeah! Helps improving family relationship. Tomorrow I will ask husband and his mom and pop to join, so all have the options to clear the positions" Another woman from the crowd said

"Right, why keep things within and suffocate self" Darshan said

Next day sharp at 5 the gathering was double than normal. First day discussion on domestic grievances allured people assemble to share and seek guidance. Saleem again in poetry mood... Fresh and energizing dawn,

Sun is opening its door to rise,
The diffident orange sphere,
Yet in semi sleep,
Snooping through cloudy veils;
For cool breeze, it was time to flow,
And ravel its cooling feel;
The blooms were bathing in cool sparkling dew;
Ants were marching one two one,
Look for food for her highness queen;
Twittering birds warbling,
From top of tree gesturing us,
"Start your yoga, we want to watch"

Shankar understood the reason of a crowd gathering. While exercising he said "as we have more new visitors, I first complement them for the session" and explained "yoga is an exercise of identifying self. It is an art of connecting body, spirit and mind together. In another way the union of body, spirit and mind is 'yoga' transforms the life pattern to kindness and spirituality. The purpose of yoga postures is to sanctify the intellect and body."

Shankar then began the topic before performing Padmasana posture "A virtuous mind, and consistency is required in this physical exercise both body and mind are involved to remain physically and mentally fit to derive ecstatic spirituality. That is why we observe who are physically fit are cool and wise."

A young girl asked "Should I say something sir"

"Yes, why not? We are here to exchange the opinions"

"Yoga is the first stage of spiritual wisdom. It prepares the body and mind to gain knowledge as who we are? And the ultimate wisdom of spirituality is cognizing the purpose of our life on earth as we will have nothing to carry back when we leave."

"Ooh! You are so young with such a vast wisdom. I salute you." Saleem was excited while saying.

Shankar sat back to perform Padmasana. With his eyes shut concentrated on his mudra directed "now you sit, elongate your legs straight and use both hands to fold right leg to place over left thigh, then fold the left leg to place along the right thigh. Bring both hands over knees with palms open then touch index fingers and thumb together. However, some use middle finger to touch the thumb. You have to be certain that you hold your head straight and back upright. Keep your eyes closed nothing in your mind except the mudra. Take long breath, hold for some time and release slowly. Repeat this exercise for 4-5 times. Sit relaxed nothing external issues in your mind, please. Now you should be perceiving energy travelling through the body. Helps blood pressure normalize, relaxes mind. The longer the posture you maintain the better for your mind and physical structure. However, don't think you can achieve in one go, you have to go stage by stage, so your mind and body endures."

For next relaxing Aasana, Shankar lay down straight along the ground then directed "Now you lie down, extending your legs straight, same position you do with your hands, put straight with palms open and eyes shut. One really significant affair for all the performers is, please do not let external force or subjects influence your mind during yoga practice, forget all. Always keep your body and mind relaxed while performing. Pose as if you are in deep sleep, as the name of this posture is 'Shavasana'. Nothing is in your mind; this exercise relieves you from stress and prepares your mind to evolve spiritually."

Finally, he thanked all participants by saying "Different paths of yoga have different objectives. However, a final objective is to know who we are and linking self with God or Super Natural force. 'Hath Yoga' physical posture to purify the body to fit for meditation. 'Karma Yoga' sacrifice, forgiveness, Compassion, caress, alms deeds are the ways to narrow the distance to reach closer to Godly world. 'Mantra Yoga' chanting universal root words for spiritual attainment. 'Bhakti yoga' total submission by submission to attain love of divinity. 'Jnana Yoga' is a path to gain wisdom through worldly spiritual knowledge. Many sages achieved this knowledge not because of reading books, but because of their endeavors of inventing and discovering worldly phenomena. 'Raja Yoga' the highest path of yoga, in other sense is called Royal or Mental Yoga. This meditation of concentration focuses minds on one point to activate inner conscious towards spirituality."

Shankar relaxed a bit before saying "now it is time we begin with social topic."

Every one curiously waited the discussion, this time even mothers in law were participants. They too wanted their grievances heard, one said "all mothers in law aren't the same and all mistakes aren't ours. We as well have married off our daughters living with mothers in law."

"It all depends on how you take the newcomer. In this entire episode woman is the enemy of woman, not men" young girl said

Yes, true, all had this opinion; one said "why women are enemies of women?" the other said

"About fifty participants of all ages would serve different opinions and would gesture who the actual perpetrator is?" Saleem anxiously uttered

"Would finally reveal an aggressive environment and the ego as a cause. The effect of the conditions drives instinct to behave." Simon instantly reverted

One married girl standing beside her in law said "Our relationship still exists cool, is all because our wave length is likewise. She knows my intention and I know her. We talk about everything, including sex that's the depth of our relationship. So I don't blame mothers in law alone"

"I don't agree, as my situation is totally different. My mother in law is devilish woman. Can't stand her a minute" A misery voice from another corner

"Marriage and my husband were the only reason for all my sufferings. But, not any more I have filed divorce from him." Another girl said a dispirited voice

A man behind her was her husband, said "It's your choice, but is no solution. You had an affair with another man, which you tried to conceal but failed. My mother while coming from office watched you both sitting in a park smooching and cohere position. Do you disagree? That is the reason my mother went against you to save me."

"I think we are going off the topic." Simon distrustfully said.

"Why not? We are discussing all, if and buts of a deteriorating relationship. The trust is the root foundation of married life. Failing this would shatter the entire family." Darshan instantly replied

"Yes, you are correct; my fault of young age too once had paralyzed my home. Things had normalized only after I convinced the wife of my mistake. The home was jittery until she forgave me." Prem pensively said

Another woman said in hesitation "for me my father in law is anathema. That rascal is a womanizer. I think nothing more need to explain why I left that house."

Shankar heard all and went down his speech "*The entire awkward situation arises as a result of upbringing in an environment that influences negativity/ positivity in one's behavior. Negative influence stimulates our negativity to rise. However, when the mind and emotional state is strongly positive, no outside negative force can act upon. Fear, greed, scruple, selfishness, ecstatic desire and impishness are evil's strategic tools to desecrate peaceful home life. Beware of its intention, its endeavor to seduce you by ephemeral ecstatic avarice.*" He took a pause to remember.

Meanwhile, everyone focused and tried to evaluate the situations behind the crisis. Most had in their mind "the atmosphere's attraction and the consciousness together link to tempt us to behave."

Shankar continued lecturing "*your home is a savor garden. Each member of a house is a variant blossom. Strews odor of variety, when you enjoy is the 'contentment'.* Evil's intensions vanish when you stick to theology in true sense whole heartedly. Pathanjali or other sages did not guide for becoming slim or enhance beauty of the face and body. But they had discovered the art of living so humans can understand the real beauty of life. Worldly gain only shoves us into the marsh."

"How does it affect the skirmishes in our homes" A lady inquired

"By yoga concentration you link mind, spirit, and body together, as I explained to you today in 'Padmasana posture'. Yoga rejuvenates your inner consciousness. You identify yourself, peace tides over you, and your inner spirit insulates you from the invasion of inequity."

A while later Shankar again said "*no one is bad, it's the thoughts that make one good or bad.* I request all mothers and daughters in law and all participants to spare some time and exercise together. Yoga together in another sense is bonded together. Many a times I have noted a lack of verbal contact fails to explore, sparks misunderstanding. So come regularly to practice yoga and see in a few months how your mind transforms to positive thoughts. Let us examine the effect in one month then we will speak on this topic."

"What about the discussion on the aging people crisis?" Prem asked

"We will discuss tomorrow after a few yoga practices."

A poem reflected in Saleem's mind "I recite my poem for all you mothers in law and daughters in law":

O' dear daughter in law... Sweetest daughter in Law,

A future mother in law too;
for me, you are princess from heaven,
Remember your first day,
first step in home,
Your bright sparkling face,
Lucid intense Aura you had;
Displayed you were no ordinary woman,
An angel from heaven to enlighten home,
You made our home blissful paradise;
My son is happy,
What else I want?
Baby granddaughter,
reminds my son's babyhood,
It's a gift I see your heart in baby,
I am you when you aren't around,
Feel warmth when taking her in arms,
My hands follow her each stage,
From crawling to walk;
I was lucky watching,
her first step walking;
I can't forget how valued you are;
When you are exhausted stressed,
Lay your head on my shoulder and sob,
Hug me hard seeking my warmth;
You were brought up in surroundings,
Different from this,

yet you attuned well,
Taught us live graceful life;
In most of homes I have seen,
Mother in laws, daughter in laws,
Two stones of grinding mill,
Son of mom and mate of woman,
Is as a piece of grain,
Gets crushed between two;
We both are women,
Have similar thoughts,
Know issues and temper of each,
Solve them when gossip together;
my dear daughter in law,
No...No its mistake,
Should say my dear daughter,
together can create an example,
How mother in law and daughter in law,
from different vicinity,
Are together as one;
Openness in alliance,
Is a way to closer ties;
Respect each other,
credible way of strengthening love;

Sun glittered shine shaping itself in the full form warming soul. All dispersed praising the poem and the topic of discussion. First day of yoga bit by bit began transforming the minds of all four friends.

They all felt a bit relaxed feeling the stretch in the knees, toe, and body "It is the best way spending time on purposeful deeds. I will ask my children in U.S and Canada to follow yoga for good health and fresh mind" Darshan said

"Good day" and all walked different directions for the day.

"A home a sweet home"

A home a sweet home,
Of a blossom garden;
Strews aroma of its bud,
Sugary nectar is for ambiance,
So are pulled to stick around,
Wander, ramble,
Where you want;
At the end it's your home,
Gives you peace and comfort,
A home a sweet home is a bond,
A place you share your heart;
The chagrin, joy, emotion or grief,
All are spices,
Add up flavor to your sweet home;
You get love and warmth,
A feel of touch,
A home is for you,
You are for home;
A home is a sweet home,
Is nest to hang out rest of the day;

Wife: A wife who enters husband's life has her own feelings and individuality. For her, marriage is an emotional tie up to live together, wish to share her feelings for emotional touch up. For her the husband/partner is not the embellishment alone, he is rather a partner, seeks to stand by with her during joy/sorrow, sweet/sour. Own home is the place for her to exhibit her personality. For a wife, husband/partner is not only the sexual partner rather he is her support, and strength. These feelings are the attractions contribute to emotions she possesses in her dream of marriage. She carries the values of married life, which she desires fulfilled through her husband. Thus, her husband is her own belonging that she never likes others to share. She would hate any intrusion and if exists, she would fight back.

- New woman enters new territory is already marked by existing reign. She may need enough intelligence and patience to manage to penetrate deep into their hearts by extending coolness.

- All mothers in law are sweet as long as don't feel a threat to their reign. By wise approach daughter in law can pull in-law's sentiments towards her to win over the endorsement. Finally, mother in law grasps the harmlessness and hands over the reign and crown.

A discord is an aggression; this is no solution as long as you have to live along. For both, estrangement, jealousy, the skirmishes are always tools of the fiend to shatter the family life. No one succeeds not even the man and the home you are fighting for.

- Wife enters new home is her submission to a new environment so she expects the support in order to sustain.

- Her relation is direct with the husband and not with others. Smooth relation with others depends on the dealings of the husband and cordial atmosphere.

- She expects a similar environment as she had in parental house. She evolved her behavior in the parental ambience are deep into her sub-conscious, cannot be changed as soon as she enters. Transformation needs zeal and love from other members of the house.

- To transform the environment, new home needs pleasant attraction so can influence to adjust. She needs her husband and a new home to understand her and her needs.

Mother: A home adorned by woman is her entity. Her own values are involved in making a home that reflects her identity. Each house interior is different from others as a result of her deep involvement to embellish to suit her taste. The woman takes special interest and calls for her feelings to ornament and organize interiors that make her soul comfortable. Woman modifies her house to fit her taste is the environment she creates that suits her and her family.

The mother who is already in control of her house would not easily give away, is the same way of politicians who hate to retreat legislation membership or seat whatever we may call. This is her mansion as she has been taken to raise the house since the start. Any challenge is the challenge to her emotions, sense of worth, identity, fondness and finally her control for own security. Therefore, she would never wish newcomer to have control on what she gathered from long-long time. This is the psychological behavior with every individual/ any life form. Who creates own territory by involving sentimentally and marks psychologically or physically to hold. Depends how species behave as human declare with outlining home, animals with other methods, declaring territory is the sensation of security. Similarly, mother too has crossed off her territory and would resist to any challenge.

An instinct as a mother emerges as soon as she is pregnant. Delivering a healthy child becomes her priority. She incurs all her efforts to protect pregnancy so the perfect child is born. The psychological change in demeanor and intense involvement convinces her into an emotional pleasure being a mother. "Going to be a mother" becomes the purpose of her life. Her preparations begin right from the first phase of pregnancy signifies how thrilled she is to have a glimpse of her new child born.

When born, is the happiest moment of her life. In summation, when called as a mother for the first time, she realizes her real uniqueness. Immediately after the birth of a child, her instinct drives her to attach the child to her body. She takes the child straight to her breast signifies that the mother is the one who is extremely and directly involved in the growth. The first milk from breast actuates the child's instinct to stay tied to the mother for the quilt. This first step conglutinates mother and child together. Her child is her soul and she would hate to detach from her because it is captivating and fulfillment for both mother and the child. She is so much involved with the child that she feels fulfilled when the child is around.

She cares for him so much that he becomes part of her life and missing a moment or a day is agonizing to her. Her care and love for him develops strong emotions and attachment. Her pain and involvement for his growth, encourages him to go closer and closer, as he finds comfort and security. She is the best friend, her lap is the best soothing refuge, her embrace is security, and her touch is relief. It is the mom everywhere and every time he needs. Therefore, intense affection with the mother encourages him to take steps favoring and pleasing her. He follows the directions of mom, assuming she is always right, what she does is for his best. It is true mother stands first for the child's glowing future.

Since the beginning mother saw him as her child. In her mind, he is still a kid, is common feelings in all mothers everywhere in the world. Mother's dominant behavior and egoistic approach with the children is to protect and secure them.

- The mother is more emotionally involved with her children than father.
- During pregnancy changes in the body create a situation of desire to undertake responsibility for carrying the child.
- Mother's warmth body is sense of contentment for a child. Therefore, always the child has a desire to cohere with the mother's body.

Son and Husband: For a Son when reaching the puberty realizes that there is something else also essential to his adult life. His necessity of carnal appetite initiates him to get attracted towards new woman. He dreams of a partner for his life and bed. A time for a new woman to enter his life, leads to the marriage or companionship. The carnal attraction for him may be for his sexual appetite. However, for the nature, it is an enticement to a human being to involve in sexual activity for creating future generation. His carnal fulfillment through a woman becomes his companion and his motivation, and whom he respected the most throughout the life is his mother. For him both wife and mother are equally important as he shares his feelings and wishes.

- For a son his mother is spiritual connection and wife is loving partner.
- For a son his mother is guidance and wife is a partner to share everything.
- For a son mother's presence is calmative and blessings and wife's presence is demulcent and fulfillment.

- Mother is a source of his existence and wife is a source to create a new generation.

- His attraction to the mother is for her sacrifices during his growth and caring nature and his attraction to the wife is sensual and fulfillment. Both are equally important for him. Proximity to one side is a spark of jealousy to another.

Prem woke up early in the morning at 4am knocked son's door. There wasn't response, knocked once again. Daughter in law 'Neelam' came out yawning and wiping her eyes "what urgency has come to wake us up?"

"Nothing, I just wanted to ask if you both wish to join a yoga class." Prem said

"Not interested" She sounded out in an annoyed feeling. But son, his name was Preetam, heard the dialogue and came out yelling in anger at his wife "Is this the way you talk to my father? You also come with us to yoga class. You need lessons."

"This is the biggest problem with you men! You can yell anytime and anywhere but we aren't allowed even to show our resentment. Is this the punishment being a woman?" She sounded out in fury again "you people don't realize the pain inside us when you doubt daughter in law's reverence" she was upset.

Somehow, Preetam managed the situation by wiping rolling tears from her eyes. Came closer, holding her tight, raised both hands to catch own ears and said "Sorry, please don't be upset. Did not mean embarrassing you"

"It's ok, but tell me, when did you finish yesterday the gossip on mother and daughter in law? How can you expect me to wake up so early when slept at 1am" Neelam sadly said

"You lovely, beautiful daughter, sweet morning is not to fight. It's my mistake awakening you early, but don't wish you skip the chance of yoga and social discussions." Prem said tranquilly

"Should I awaken kids?" Prem then went inside. Kids normally loved sleeping with Grandfather's for angel and butterfly stories.

"Are you an idiot? Don't you know I am in period? How can you expect me to perform exercise" Neelam rapped out quietly

"You know better to manage" Preetam said silently

A few moments later the kids were in Prem's arms, eyes were still shut resisting grandpa's lure of candy. Finally, all got ready to move.

Sharp early at 5am all reached. Simon, Saleem and Darshan were already present. Dawn was tempting cool. All assembled, crowd was more than the last days. All wanted the Yoga and preach to surrender to spiritual nature and its lucidity.

Saleem sniffing cool adores of breeze recited a poem:

Partly woken sun,
Snooping through cloudy blind;
Clouded maritus and clouded marita,
Magic negative, positive making love;
Silent drops of carnalis,
Enthralling birds,
Singing songs of love,
Blossom petals are wet,
Liberating fervent savor,
Go and amuse worldly life;
Stimulating papilios,
Spreading wings and dance;
Beetles making tickling move,
Gesturing love your nature,
It's all yours, you have;
No car, no fashion,
No stuff, can replace,
It's all free for you,
Love it and live it;

Shankar bowed his head joining both palms together "Namaste. Today, after we warm up a bit will learn kundalini yoga. The aged, weak and girls wearing sari may avoid participating this exercise as is bit stressful."

To warm up, he suggested to do bhujangasana also good for all ages "lie flat along your stomach, forehead resting on the ground and toes flat on the ground holding your legs tightly together. Put your hands below the shoulder, keeping your elbows parallel and close to your body. Take a deep breath in; slowly lift your head, chest and abdomen while keeping your navel on the floor. Put the same amount of pressure on your palms. Pull your torso back and off the ground with the support of your hands. This exercise is also known as cobra pose, as rises above the ground to display aggressive neck ribs into flattened hood. Continue breathing with awareness, as you curve your spine vertebra by vertebra. If possible, straighten your arms by arching your back as much as possible; tilt your head backwards and face upward. Breath out, gently bring your abdomen, chest and head back to the floor. Don't overstretch or overstrain yourself. During whole exercise smile makes easier doing and easy breathing comforts practicing posture."

Before going to kundalini yoga he stated an example "*It's a saying, negative is an electric shock, don't touch until you have rubber gloves in hand. Insulate yourself to all negativity that comes to drive you on. The insulation is your positivity thwarts negative's attempt, and you win. This is the teaching 'be positive even in negative reign'.*"

Neelam was quite impressed by the preaching asked "Can you kindly elaborate, so we can understand more?" With curiosity she looked at his face in smile expecting his detailed dialect.

"*Both negative and positive are essential phenomena of the universe. Though both are different identities opposite to each other, yet are tempted to bond together. The outcome of their connection is 'reaction'. The reaction is the crucial factor to produce universal values. Each example we witness, has two sides, one matches us and the other mismatches. What matches, we call positive and other as negative. Does not mean what doesn't match you, mismatches all. Hence the negative for you, many a times is positive for others, however, depends on the conditions you sustain.*"

Shankar paused for a while to find an example to quote "For instance, a wretched man in acute hunger has not fed for several days accepts only one objective, come what may need to satisfy the belly. Would seek whatever means to fill his belly as his priority is to allay hunger. His hunger forces him to beg, pick from dirt, steal, or seek whatever means. There the positivity isn't to keep away from corrupt means, but rather to satisfy hunger. It may be negative for us as we have enough food to eat."

High court Judge 'Iyyer' from the crowd assented saying "I agree as I witnessed several poor begging and picking leftover food outside restaurants, very sad".

———

The judge 'Iyyer' was born in a small village of Tanjavur in Tamil Nadu to a very poor farmer. Sometimes food two times a day and sometimes had to content with one time. The economic apathy of the father persuaded him to work as a helper in the temple that added to family income. After working for some years in temple he learnt a lesson to 'have faith'.

One day when the priest was free, he got a chance to ask "why some are poor and some so rich?"

Impressed by the child's query the priest looked at his face then dabbed his cheek while saying "*You are poor because the other one is rich. I think this example will clear you: We have two pieces of bread if equally shared, both have same amount of bread to eat, is called parallelism. On the other hand if the person takes away 1 ½ of two pieces is called imparity. The situation exists* in where the economic system of production and the distribution is based on competition, the stronger one takes advantage and the weaker fails. Both have advantages and disadvantages, however, when both reach extreme, starts misbalancing the results."

The priest then looked at watch in his wrist "'O' already half past ten" went inside to get some money "I am hungry, go and get some idli for our brunch"

The child Iyyer received money from him and walked away to the restaurant. Back in 10 minutes with Idli and separately in small poybags saambar, coconut mixed horse gram chatni. Went inside to clean plantain leaves and fetched glasses, laid a leaf on the floor, placed a glass with water on his right. Placed Idlis in flat leaf laid on ground and poured saambar and chatni over. Both sat on the floor, folded both legs over each. Both took some water to sprinkle before incanting "satyam tvartena parishincAmi" meaning in English - O Food! You are true. I encircle you with Divine righteousness."

After finishing the brunch the priest came back to the preaching "where were we?"

"Then why parallelism isn't adopted? So all have equal share!" The child Iyyer asked

"Because the struggle to survive is in the blood, saving is an instinct drives them to source more for future use. If you have observed animals in the forest, dig a pit to hide the left over, clears how instinct drives species." The priest said

Though for the young child was tough to understand yet he tried to grasp and said "it's the survival instinct, which influences our behavior. But there is difference between other species and the humans. Other species look for food only when they are hungry, on the other hand humans are always hungry"

The priest observed his heart burn, answered "It wasn't there in antiquity. Needs were limited to food, clothing and the shelter. But over the time as a result of evolution of trade avarice too ascended"

"Accumulation becomes the priority and purpose of life insignificant" the young Iyyer said

We have both negative and positive aspects in each discernible object or ambiance, both have to reach to extreme as dawn to torrid noon and lastly dusk to dark night, because new day has to come" the priest said

"Why richness is not the victim of negative sphere?" child Iyyer asked

"It's because poverty is the negative to richness. One is rich because has sought the other's share to add in one's deposit. As already explained, happens in the competition of survival. The struggle to secure future prompts to accumulate as much as possible. Sometimes the tendency to accumulate coerces to accept both legal and illegal means. Seeking fallacious methods to conceal or victimize people to amass is sin. Each religious inscription also says this. Doesn't mean all adopt unacceptable means to get rich. Many are rich as a result of positive thinking" the priest answered

Child Iyyer's curiosity persuaded to ask "How negativity effect is made ineffective?"

"*The system is the basis that pulls habitants to integrate into it. Majority of the people of the society who follow create atmosphere. Those fail to follow are failures*" the priest said

"How can majority of people change the ambiance?" Child Iyyer asked

"Good observation, I give an example: In a group of fifteen, ten think positive and five opposite. The majority will have their say heard than the minority. Same way the negativity is transforms to positivity."

"Can you please elaborate more on this?" The child Iyyer asked

"*In each negative atmosphere there is a daring person to open the door from negative side. Enduring the ferocity closely makes him resistant enough to prepare mass to follow to join the race for transformation. The person, who opens the door, is called 'leader' or 'Icon'*" the priest guided

"You mean ferocity impels negativity!" child Iyyer said observing spiritual facet of priest's guidance

"Yes sure, but don't forget, *the positivity rises from the marsh of the negativity as lotus rises in sludgy pond*" the priest guided

"Then why can't we emerge out of negativity?" Child asked again

"*The negative is the surface where lies the first step of ladder to positive. When you succeed to scale the first step, the next stages, step by step become effortless.*" The priest said while dabbing his hand

"But how? I don't see any way out" the child Iyyer inquired

"*First you learn to endure negative atmosphere. You will observe strong metaphysical insulation coat around you to thwart the negativity. That actuates you to realize there is another world. You find when you defeat negative*" boosting his morale the priest said.

Young Iyyer found interesting preaching "Why things transform from one stage to another?"

The priest was impressed by his observation, gave a lesson "nothing is immortal, all have to wither one day as we in old age"

The preaching began to transform his wisdom. He had never expected such a lesson from middle aged priest, asked "But why people step into old age?"

"Each species and plant has to experience each stage of life, the infancy, childhood, puberty, middle age and finally the old age as prepares to leave the space for new one to occupy. A fruit initially is tasteless, then sour, sour and sweet and finally sweet. But when sweetness reaches an extreme, begins to rot to land on earth to fertile and sow seeds on the ground for new life. Similarly the old age is for an end of physical life. As, spirit as a seed for new life inscribed in 'Rig *Veda 10.4.57.4: Many of your spirits return again, to perform pure acts for exercising strength, and to live long and to see the sun'.* Though it is still indistinct to me, nevertheless, my assumption is, there is something beyond our life, as we aren't the battery operated toys or robots. We are a perfect creation of the unknown with a purpose, maybe for energy or for something else, no evidence to prove yet."

Child Iyyer started thinking the stages in life and the beyond but wasn't reaching anywhere near to conclusion. The deeper he penetrated into life the more confusion he confronted. The depth of wisdom was the ocean, the deeper he swam, the more the distance he found. There was no end to it. Then he thought better to concentrate in present life, asked "Why aged are weaker than in their younger life?"

"Because you have accomplished the duties, tools are no more needed. Thus, wither day by day. The soul through the experiences has gained what it had to. Now back to infancy (weak old age) rely on others to walk, talk, eat and hear" the priest explained

"Seems eerie, Do all have to go this stage?" The child Iyyer asked

"Depends how long you live. Yes, you enjoy when you have company to share warmth, physical and mental support" the priest explained

"What happens to them who don't have family support" child Iyyer asked

"I give my example: I have no woman no child, I'm brahmachari and priest, devoted all my life to God. But in my old age, I need someone like you for support. During walk, lay my hand around your shoulder and in my last day of life your lap to lay my head. Do you agree?"

"Yes sir, it's my honor" the Iyyer child said.

The turning point reached Iyyer's door step. He learnt a lot from that sage who made him study in the school. The childhood struggle to survive made him stronger and stronger to fight back the negativity of poverty. Once heard the proverb from his the priest preceptor *"each day a new day because new day has new lessons"*. He found the negativity as his lesson to rise stage by stage.

29

Those souvenirs preaching were the steps of his ladder. Above all, the priest taught him to respect the aged.

———

A young boy agreeing said "the man already gripped by negativity has no choice left but to accept negative means is positive for him as Negative plus Negative is positive."

Some laughed for this joke, but some hailed saying "yes Negative plus Negative is Positive. But who is responsible for this negativity?"

The theme was getting off so Shankar drew attention of all by saying "*The circumstances are the game changer that influences our mind through its negative and positive values. However, if the positivity dominates your individuality, foils the motive of negative atmosphere. Therefore, the spiritual exercises insulate us from negative invasion.*"

Somehow, the preaching was confusing to Neelam, held her head, pondered over and over to understand. Shankar read her confused face and said "I think you are not clear!" He paused for a while to find examples to explain "Ok, how do you feel when you sit in a beautiful garden with the variety odor of flowers?"

"Phrenetic, delights the soul and thoughts for cool." Neelam said

"But when you visit a burial of your close friend, how do you feel?" Shankar asked

"Totally opposite" Neelam replied. She was getting the point and said "Got it, environment or surroundings influence us to behave in accordance with the situation."

"For you, burial gave negative feelings and blossom garden gave positive. Both have the capacity to influence to achieve their objectives. Nevertheless, people react in accordance with the (+ -) negative - positive qualities in possession. Sometimes even blossomed garden and burial place fail to influence. It's all because negative or positive phenomena in your identity is stronger than surroundings influence" Shankar said

"But how? In burial place no one laughs and in blossomed garden no-one feels sad" Neelam remarked

"When you are already depressed inside by some serious tragic incidence, the blossomed park won't ravish you. On the other side, who already scorns the dead man may not be equally sad as others. It's entirely because the negativity in possession while meeting occurrences" Shankar explained

"I think it is clear now. *Negative, positive in individuality and in the environment connect together and dominant one conquers the weak to thwart or give in. Forgiveness, compassion, gratitude and faith in God are the positivity to transform a person.*" Neelam said

Shankar sought permission from all "we will discuss this afterwards, now it's time to yoga practice"

All got ready, waiting to practice the physical lessons of Yoga.

"Kundalini yoga is most suited to transform behavior and defeats addiction. Lay flat your back touching ground. Inhale slowly as you pull the lower belly to lift your leg up 90 degrees and toes stretching upwards. Nothing except the exercise is in your head. Your lower back may have some strain; in that case, place your hands under hips for extra support. Exhale slowly as you lower the leg down. Repeat, left and right leg lifting upwards alternately for at least 3 minutes. You will sense the energy flowing towards the brain." He stopped for a while to help others to relax. "We are going for next 12 postures of kundalini yoga."

One by one all went through the exercises. However, he had to halt as all were exhausted.

Among gathered were some aged women who, having learned from neighboring groups, purposely approached to address their grievances.

One woman of age 85 unable to walk was supported by the neighboring women. Her pale and drawn face, dry tear drops, finding space to drift out of sunken eyes, clearly gestured her anguish, said in a vague weeping voice "I am 85 now; both my sons have died 2 and 3 years back. The home of 3 bedroom set I had presented to my son ten years back at a time everything was lovely. Even daughter in law had a cordial relation, was always supportive. All of a sudden after my son's death, the situation had worsened at her demand of 2 hundred thousand rupees cash I have in my bank."

She held edging of her sari and wiped tears rolling down, said in the plaintive sound "What is the assurance that she will take care of me even after I hand over all my money? On my refusal, she pushed me out of the home. Now I survive in exposed territory, only help from some of the neighbors. I have no old age pension, no old age home, not even medicines. Tell me where shall I start? Whose door I knock? Many a time's thoughts came into my head, why God does not get me out from this inferno. What sin I did to endure pain in this old age."

The atmosphere in the group had shifted to misery. Some touched her feet, some kissed her and some held her hand to soothe. But was no resolution to that suffering.

Before Shankar could speak anything a middle aged man came forward with his colleague advocate friend. "Sir, I am a Judge and my friend is a famous lawyer. We will manage this situation and will address you the status."

Shankar asked "But how?"

The Advocate read out the book which he carried with him "the Maintenance and Welfare of Parents and Senior Citizens Act, 2007 chapter ii: maintenance of parents and senior citizens

1. A senior citizen, including a parent who is unable to maintain himself from his own earning or property owned by him, shall be entitled to make an application under section 5 in case of-

    i.   parent or grand-parent, against one or more of his children not being a minor

    ii. a childless senior citizen, against such of his relative referred to in clause (g) of section 2

2. The obligation of the children or relative, as the case may be, to maintain a senior citizen extends to the needs of such citizen so that senior citizen may lead a normal life.

3. The obligation of the children to maintain his or her parent extends to the needs of such parent either father or mother or both, as the case may be, so that such parent may lead a normal life.

4. Any person being a relative of a senior citizen and having sufficient means shall maintain such senior citizen provided he is in possession of the property of such senior citizen or he would inherit the property of such senior citizen:

Provided that where more than one relatives are entitled to inherit the property of a senior citizen, the maintenance shall be payable by such relative in the proportion in which they would inherit his property."

Another aged man tried to voice his grievances "Sir, please help me from daughter in law and her children. I have no pension and I have to endure all persecutions. She scolds, sometimes without food, uses all tactics to throw me out of the house. My dumb son watches with no resistance."

The Judge said to the aged man, "Sir, if your plight is genuine. We definitely will support you."

He immediately acted to collect the details for action under the Senior Citizens Act, 2007. Then both before leaving to reach the court timely said "*we need to*

find ways to restore elderly values in our country. We exist because of them. The old age is our future; we have to fight right from now."

The other girl from the bunch said "the aged are as good as kids so they need love and respect."

Shankar pronounced "I recite a few verses of religious scriptures: *(Quran 17:23-24): "Your Lord has commanded that you worship none but Him, and that you be kind to your parents. If one of them or both of them reach old age with you, do not say to them a word of disrespect, or scold them, but say a generous word to them. And act humbly to them in mercy, and say, 'My Lord, have mercy on them, since they cared for me when I was small.'"*

(Leviticus 19:32): "'Stand up in the presence of the aged, show respect for the elderly and revere your God. I am the LORD." (Ephesians 6:1-3): "Children, obey your parents in the Lord, for this is right. "Honor your father and mother"—which is the first commandment with a promise— 'so that it may go well with you and that you may enjoy long life on the earth."

(Manu Samhita (MS:2.121): He who habitually salutes and constantly pays reverence to the aged obtains an increase of four (things), (viz.) Length of life, knowledge, fame, (and) strength. (MS2.119-120): One must not sit down on a couch or seat which a superior occupies; and he who occupies a couch or seat shall rise to meet a (superior), and (afterwards) salute him. For the vital airs of a young man mount upwards to leave his body when an elder approaches; but by rising to meet him and saluting he recovers them.

(Matthew 19:19): Honor your father and mother, and, you shall love your neighbor as yourself." (Timothy 5:1-3): Do not rebuke an older man harshly, but exhort him as if he were your father. Treat younger men as brothers, [2] older women as mothers, and younger women as sisters, with absolute purity.

(Buddha said): "Mata pitu upatthanam etam mangalam uttamam" - means supporting parents is a great blessing. Having good parents, kind-hearted parents, is really a very great blessing to a family, a great fortune.

The majority of us go each day to temples, churches and mosques, listen to preachers, read the Quran, Bible, Torah, Granth and Veda. My question is how far are we sincere to the religious inscriptions? Why do we go to religious places and read religious scriptures? All is waste until we loyally follow the guidelines. Had we loyally followed sacred books we could have averted the deploring situation."

Many women and men's heads crouched in shame. "We are disrespecting our religions and scriptures." Darshan was emotional while saying.

"Modern world does not care to understand the religious book inscription. They only brag, to be known by the people they are religious and read holy books." A postgraduate in philosophy from the crowd said

"I doubt materialism is equally responsible for disrespecting aged. I have one daughter and three sons. None of my sons wish to hold me in his house. Each one wants to pass the burden to another. All this is because; I have no wealth to tempt them. Three sons can't care one parent, but one parent relishes even the pain while taking care of all kids. This is the verity" Saleem was agonized while saying

A woman of middle age stood up sobbing and tears in her eyes said "I live with my husband with 3 kids and aged mother in law. For several days he never returned home pretending day and night work. However, my doubts persuaded to follow his motions and found he had illicit relationship with 2 other women. After getting caught he sought violence to silence me. Nowadays he avoids me, beats me and kids, and never even gives money for expenses. I can't stand any more. It was blunder trusting him to leave my job. Never had support from the mother in law, even in the event he wants to kick me out of his house." She waited a minute, wiped her tears with edging of a sari, and said again in hissing sound "where do I begin? What do I do? I am frightened for me and my kids."

Her soulful issue drew attention of the entire crowd. People whispered sympathetically for this ungodly deed of a man responsible. "None should desert a woman who left her job to take care of his children. Bringing up a child is a more difficult task than any chore in this world. He considers a woman as a sex toy, doesn't catch the mother hidden behind. We should not spare such people. We will support her in all sense."

The advocate advised her "Economically he is liable to bear all your and kids' expenses. Kicking out a wife legally married or a girlfriend living for long isn't that easy. Both mutually have to reach agreement before the court for any separation. You can seek police assistance for his violent acts. Please tell this to your husband who harasses you. Law in all sense is for protecting wife, but most women fail as a result of their regard and honor to the husband and fear of humiliation in the society. However, seeking separation is your last option as will affect the kids psychologically. May be, they already have begun experiencing as a result of domestic violence. As for your mother in law, she will never have voice as long as she is economically dependent. So blaming her may not be justified."

The advocate again said "I will have Domestic violence act 2005 and Senior citizen act 2007 copies delivered to all the members of our league. It's a shame we are unaware of our rights. Lack of information prompts enduring sufferings. Go to site 'e-filing supreme court of India' and file your genuine complaint. If you want our help we are there. If you wish, we will visit your home after our league is registered. Have patience for a week or ten days."

"Marriage dream fails when"

Marriage is portrayed as kismet, people wait anxiously for this moment to enter married life. Celebrations and custom rituals add up spices to more tasteful marriage. Dreams of Selfness of having own family and kids are the first choice.

Each single, whether man or woman possesses a dream and expectations for his/her future partner to look and behave like princes/prince and so in the dream that comes true is the fortune for one. Nevertheless, normally dreams don't come true in many instances, as dreams are different from reality. In real life, there is a great deal of difference in external look and the experiences of practical life.

My experiences contacting couples reflects both are opposite to each other in behavior, in many incidences this behavioral change contributes to uncomfortable positions for each other. Behavioral modification in a man or woman is caused by the temperament possessed and the part played in the house, which creates the environment to act and respond. For example, requirement of a woman is the necessities for feeding the family and man's is to arrange those needs. Both are different objectives though for one purpose, a woman will not be able to operate a household without the required arranged by a man. Besides this role, man and woman have an important role of emotional and physical care for each other. Giving importance to the partner's role and involve intensely meeting his/her role in the house promotes understanding each other. Intense interest in the family affairs motivates to sacrifice, averts many problems of marital life. Major points as I feel for both husband and wife to keep married life intact are:

1. Dreams are far-far away from the real life, accepting the truth would benefit from actual life.

2. High expectation from the partner is the root to disappointments and frictions. Treat the partner as human.

3. The deep involvement of a partner in the family affairs keeps away the attention elsewhere. Endeavors to be to take the partner emotionally and physically.

4. Respect the identity and integrity of a spouse. This develops likeness, understanding, and submission emotionally.

5. Emotional and physical care of the partner is the magnet for attracting attention.

6. Sexual attraction is a tool to pull partner towards you. It is equally necessary as food and water for a healthy couple, enough and delicious sexual life at home would discourage looking for alternate.

Each person has own identity and quality, the personal identity is reflected through communication and activities. Major behavior which affects married life is Negative/ Positive, Introverted/ extroverted and strong/ weak, these characters control us. In some negative dominates and in some positive dominates, and what dominates reveals through reaction. As I observed, there is almost no house where the wife says my husband is perfect also the opinion of the husband is same for his wife. Hence, one has to agree as no one is perfect, need an endeavor to exploit for the objective of union. The strong point of marriage rests on how you see and respond to the partner's behavior. If both partners understand each other, react in accordance would avoid clashes and violence. In each household there are opinion differences; to make out is the caliber of both spouses:

1. To extinguish fire, water or other cool substance is the option. To be cool when find the possibility of arguments and settle the thing in the proper surroundings. Arguments become clash and then differences in the partnership only accelerate distasteful married life, is one of the causes of infidelity.

2. Many couples do not like each other's odor rather cannot stand, in such cases during sleep any important discussion may result to arguments. Because is already riled by the distaste of odor to give a confident answer.

3. Many small-pity incidences like he/she does not dress well, very slow, does not clean well, does not smile, talk too much or too serious and etc., Together form a big consolidated issue, when minded and stored in self stimulates dislike towards partner.

4. In many houses, arguments begin with cursing each other for not doing this or done that, is normally stimulated by the development of dislike of prior incidences. In families dominant people's stubbornness pursues partner to behave opposite when patience reaches beyond sufferance. Such people are too extroverted and negative, which prevents them calculating others mind. They deliver a feeling what they feel is appropriate. No one is same and each one possesses intelligence. One is good at kitchen and another in arranging. Avoiding comparison softens relation.

5. Women are more emotional than men. Women use heart to think and Men use brain. So women need emotional touch up, attention and presence recognized.

A relationship is successful as long as the attraction between the partners is intact. Attraction of actions, attentiveness, beauty, behavior, embrace, sexual satisfaction and etc, contribute to prolong association.

Activities to attract partner slows down over time as becomes generic daily routine. Especially in middle age the temptation and the attraction gradually droops, persuades for something new. Some come down into this marsh, but some fail the devil's intension to secure family life.

A person has two main roles in married life, one for the spouse and the other is the resources to manage the house. The partner and the family attraction influence to conduct responsibilities to benefit the family. Therefore, the involvement in responsibilities intensifies resulting lapses attentiveness to the spouse. Especially most women undergo this stage involving intensely in free services of taking guardianship of children and bringing off the household.

After returning from the office male partner expects his wife fresh and sexy who is already heavily weighted down by hardship. Man does not understand the situation she has undergone since morning till he arrives. Here both expect soothing caress from each other, but no-one is serious. Expectations of both fail. A disappointment is the major factor of fading attraction. The men too face same situation when they deeply involve themselves in their responsibilities in the office or elsewhere. Failure to dedicate time to family or wife is the serious complaint, the woman in the house does not grasp his issues, thus blames husband for the negligent conduct. Both become responsible for weakening relation.

Fading attraction drives to tilt towards fresh and new attractions so can fill what is missing. Those who are exposed to external surroundings are easily drawn into these draws.

Each adult female or male is exposed to external atmosphere, is obligated to hate or approve one of many he/she in contact. The instinct of an individual influences to observe and analyze other's personality as good or bad or 'so-so' (look, personality, action and etc ;). In all conditions of yes or no have the ability to attract or repel. One to like and another to despise, 'so-so' characters generally lack to attract deeply is normal behavior. Escaping from this situation is impossible as the brain reacts instantly to look out for right or wrong. The approval indicates the acceptance of personality that matches own.

In the offices or other outside connections, meet both sexes. Working men and females spend more on working hours than staying with the mates. Spend most of their day with them eating, chatting, and joking, etc.; these develop a warm relationship to step further to go closer. Working individual of strong character having a happy married life limits to move forward. Individuals having shattered married life are tempted to get closer as long as getting contentment missing in the home. On the other hand, weak characters are well motivated to luxury of emotions irrespective of family atmosphere.

However, no one can stop imagining the dominant personality of fellow workers or remote links means colleague's personality to influence enough to memorize and reverie. Now working woman/ man maintains relationships with two, one physical relation and the other in imagination.

The comparison of partner and the colleague begins, ambiance effect of household and spouse if is stronger he/she inclines towards home and if not the passion starts with the colleague. Colleague's initiation helps to establish unions, some manage secret relation and some dares break up an existing relationship.

Sexual appetite is essential want of an adult. Some are content and some have great craving, for them controlling sexual appetite is really unmanageable. They assuage their hunger through others. Most women control desire despite inadequate sexual appetite in fear of social consequences, responsibility towards kids and family insecurity.

Reasons for a woman and man to get involved in extramarital relationships may be as I feel:

1. Powerful emotional and physical attraction of a stranger or other associate pulls the mind and heart to submit.

2. Dissatisfaction and boring emotional and physical relation with partner.

3. Lack of motivation for deep involvement in family activities.

4. Fading spouse's sexual attraction is a tone to establish extramarital relations.

5. For a woman it is also sometimes revenging the spouse in cruel relation.

6. Genetic characteristics of individual for emotional and sexual desire for more sex, addiction, curiosity, draws opposite sex's attention to become special and variety. These denote the weakness of the person.

7. Weak and submissive behavior to submit to other's intentions.

It is lifelike that no one would wish partner to share sexual emotions with someone else, it hurts and renders pain as both are assets of each other. Relation breaks, one prefers not to abide together with dishonest companion unless one is so grateful to forgive and forget the dishonesty.

As long as there are wife and husband and marriage; extra marital relation will be illicit – deceitful and will be called "infidelity". For both wife and husband, it is an issue of dependability, emotional security, bond of togetherness. Adult females are more concerned as a family is their security, togetherness is soothing touch. All family life and family's future shatters in case of any one switch to extra marital relation. Most of us don't realize the aftermath, yet indulge into such activities that damages children and happy family life.

For some it is a mistake, but for those who relied and trusted is severe incurable injury, over and over refreshes. Many realize late and look for the reasons the reasons as why did she/he go for it? Was he/she not happy? If not, why not? What I or children could have done for it? One must make each day a new day with new attractions. That is the reason many women in the home add, detract, modify, retouch the objects and shift from one spot to some other. This is one path to the partner's attention to applaud her attempts. Nevertheless, sometime goes opposite still it is attraction to involve at home. Attraction of kids allures the companion. Men and Women find ways to do something new to same old house brings freshness for lasting memory. I feel some as:

1. In order to avoid partner diverting mind invite and motivate his/her deep involvement in family activities.

2. Revitalize the faded attraction of home and self this is magnet prevents from thinking others. Lifeless homes are not places.

3. Before getting sucked up to others thinking about home and kids will restrict distrustful action.

4. The emotional involvement of the partner towards family by reminding responsibilities and emotional touch up.

5. Psychological treatment of weak character of sexually addicted spouse.

6. Respect the identity and integrity of a spouse.

7. Wrong and cruel atmosphere of the home is instigation to go for better.

8. Many adult females in the offices are influenced by bosses for sexual favors. This uncommon behavior is common in many offices. Under these circumstances husband is best to advise to tackle the situation, risking job is no matter if husband prefers to handle legally with such masses.

"Love life is happy married life"

A young man of 30 working in BPO blushed while saying "I work in a call center and spend 12-15 hours in the work place. Later on a tiring day in the office, I reach home at around 9pm to watch my wife's awful face. We are economically sound, have mostly everything what a family wants. But many a times I disappoint her when we are in bed. She blames and suspects my illicit relationship with other women. To my honesty, my wife is my childhood friend. How can I cheat her, knows me from bottom to top, same I too. I love her, but inability to satisfy her dispirits me. Only I know how much courage I gathered to speak out my sexual problem, all because I don't want to lose her." The wan face and red wet eyes revealed his anguish in order to pull through his relation"

"Are we not off the topic? What connection does it have, nonsense?" Priya blushed while saying

"May sound vulgar, but has a major role to bond wife and husband together. Happy family is a way to happy home" the doctor advised

A young man of BPO said again "she is always stressed fights with my pop and mom, turns violent even in pity incidences. She was never like this before. I know my weakness, what I do not to overcome"

"You must take her to the doctor" a voice from the crowd

Shankar looked at young man in appreciation and said "Sexual weakness is being faced by several young males and females but they don't come out easily. You have done a good job for others. Modern greedy needs and economic insecurity, together compel to stressful life, suppresses the sexual readiness. Sexual activity is strongest spiritual yoga, a law of divinity for procreation. To move on, you need to give up your excessive material aspirations. Eventually, a man needs woman, and woman a man. All men and women have dreams before and during knot to married life. Sex is the foundation of married life; you should master to gratify spouse's fervor. She needs your embracement and caress to quench her emotional drive."

Shankar explained again after taking a sip of water "In order to maintain the drive in you, you need to follow essential points. For best bedtime moments focus on few points:

I.   Don't hang on to stress for longer time. When such situation comes up, think the positive side and relax.

II. Discuss with her whole day activity and get involved for solution. She will feel half of mental burden relieved.

III. Healthy timely food to avoid gastric.

IV. Sleep well and drink good amount of water each day. Good sleep helps to remain fresh and more you drink water more you go for urine that helps releasing toxins and unwanted elements.

V.   Fresh mind so no other thinking invades you. The mind is everything to drive desire, brain functioning, creation of ambiance, and submission.

VI. Submission is very important next to desire. As the moment, you discharge semen you are totally submitted to its release.

VII. Desire; as long as you have no desire you cannot function. Desire prompts the brain to direct heart and blood to act faster.

VIII. Sexual arousal is as a result of increase of heart rate and blood pressure. Heart pumps faster so blood moves faster than average to warm organs to erectile condition.

IX. Caress each other, till you both arouse, she too is human. Spend some 10-15 minutes on romantic discussions before you prepare.

X.   Avoid too much drinking and smoking.

XI. Make sure you both enjoy equally. Do whatever she wants, right from face and breast as she desires arousal before action.

XII. Same old method is always boring so choose fresh methods as Kama sutra guides.

XIII. Both mind and body are the participants to fulfil the needs. Mind Stress less and body strong enough to perform. If physical issue, better consult a doctor as depression most of times kills not only sexual urge but also causes mental fatigue.

Normally, most people lack to understand the importance of sexual contentment, this is the essential glue to bond companion together. In many houses fanatical approach towards women partner fails to see the need of adult females. Quenching sensual urge pulls both together to cohere as one. Your wave length, mutual respect and understanding instinctively show up.

To prepare sharing bed, relieve all your stress. First make your spouse sit close to you touching your body and direct to do the same you do. Chat romantic for a few minutes and embellish by touching. Then sit straight folding your legs. Make sure no office or economic activity is in your head. Hold spouse's hand then place between her folded legs. And meditate for 5-10 minutes you will experience your warm energy travelling through her torso. Continue till she too feels warmth."

Another aged man stood up to explain his plight "I am an aged 65 living alone, after separation from wife and almost in divorce situations. Even my kids don't want me though I lived for them all my life. They say I never loved them. My entire struggle day and night was to fulfill dreams of family's comfort and the rise of kids. Though didn't evince what I possessed in my heart for them. I believed 'love is karma shown by deeds and not by manifestation'." His eyes were wet and red sobbed consistently though wished to say, but the tongue and the lips were weak. Some sitting beside him stood for comfort and made him sit. A few minutes later he recited the poem of plight:

Love is 'Karma' shown by deeds;

I am your father,
earning member of home;
Woke up early,
Came late at night,
Went to work,
When you were asleep,
came late at home,
when you were asleep;
Many a times missed your touch,
But solaced again and again,
My hard work shall pay one day;
My Journey was so hard,
raising you and home;
Never could spare a moment,
Thinking me and my future life;
All my past, present and future,
Was you and your mom;
But something drove into dark,
We broke apart,
Hearts and soul severed;
Doesn't mean,
All I lost from my heart;
don't you ever turn back?
as I am no longer with your mom;
Father too is someone,
Who cares kid the most,
But failed to display,
Love inside me for you;
My love was your rise in life,
My love was you live a happy life;
I don't expect too much from you,
Only consider giving,
Little space in your heart,
So I am remembered as your pride;
Father too loves his kids,
But can't simply waste time,

Live and let live

Displaying heart full of love;
Love is 'Karma' shown by deeds;
Don't simply consider me,
As father because your mother said so;

"Yes, true for all kids, the mothers are first and fathers are used as spare parts" middle aged man spoke from the crowd.

"It's because the mother is a close friend of kids. She always stays with them even in absence, to share all bad and good, ifs and buts." A lady said

"Oh Come on! Most fathers always are portrayed among children as a scary stuff" A man said

A woman thought for a moment, confessed "Yes, sometimes we seek father as a tool to scare kids as kids don't listen to us as a result of our closeness. This doesn't mean we misguide kids about the earning member and the leader of a house. Kids should have a fear of someone for their misconduct. The father we use as a caveat. This does not distance them from father. Whenever, father has a off from office, its celebration at my home."

Another man said in fuming voice "In my house the situation is similar. Men right early in the morning with lunch box move for the office. Unaware of a wife plotting against them work hard and harder and hand over salary. A husband is as good as dog for her. Dog's service is needed as long as she wants. As long as he twitches his tail, he is good; the day he revolts his days are numbered. She masterminds the plot in such a way that even kids say the father is fiend."

A middle age lady said "this is ridiculous. Shut up"

He turned his face back and found she was his wife "I will not stop! I have to tell more... What is the reason behind avoiding me, you have to explain now?"

"Because, you always come drunk in the house and yell at me. Children are scared of you. I have also noticed your relationship with another woman"

"Oh come on you lady! How can you accuse anyone without any firm evidence," he pronounced

"The evidence is long hair on your shirt collar, not once but several times. All women will hate such person," she pronounced

He thought for some time and came to the conclusion. His suspicion on colleague's prank for fun was correct "How can you inculpate like this. Hair may be of mom or yours or the girl of my child's age sits next to me in the office. Does this mean I had involved in carnal connection with that girl. Aren't you ashamed?"

"If true, though I still doubt, why don't you engage with me? Some men don't understand what a woman wants" She again stated

"You must say... I can't always behave like a dog for your needs"

Live and let live

Losing his control in anger again yelled "The situation could have been defused, but rather you preferred to ignite. You are boorish."

"Don't shout at me" the disgrace coerced her to crouch down.

In the same tone he said again "One more point I want to tell you, never suspect unless you have solid evidence. This only adds fuel to fire."

Staring her face, he said "whenever I am at home first thing I encounter is your grunt, gives the headache to me. I may not earn enough, but whatever I earn hand over to you."

The irritated wife started sobbing said "You are humiliating me in public"

"Oh... Woman always tears ready to come out. You are too canny, beyond my imagination."

"If I fight, is for I chose you as my lifelong companion. What you mean, I should beg for the contentment" She said in deploring voice

The igniting atmosphere by diverging arguments between him and the woman wasn't ending. However, in many houses suspicions too was one among the causes of domestic crisis. Shankar intervened to cool down the place. However, he did not want to touch this topic as was very sensitive and could hurt many. He preferred to change the topic.

Shankar explained, watching the lamenting woman "*Trust is the foundation of all relationships. A relationship is like love marsh, has the ability to drown in. Both are responsible to attract each other to retain pleasing home ambience, so lasts even when away from domicile. When both live together each has a liability to caress the other. Some persons aren't content with what they own; wander hither and thither to look for happiness without realizing the happiness comes up from within. Search inside self, you will find what you need. Love you find when you know love. Wandering for love is no love; it only shoves you towards skepticism and disloyalty. Also eludes failures in handling responsibilities. Enduring sufferings makes you stronger and stronger. Be cool and don't be scared, learn to face it, sufferings will fail one day. Power to defeat the negativity is the competence*"

Some other lady said "Don't weigh all women in one weighing machine. I and my husband are of the same wavelength, as easily as a virtuous unpriced dilettante. Seek emotional and spiritual security through him. He is a partner with whom I can share all my joy and grief. For me sexual appetite is important, but isn't as important as I gain emotional touch up through him. I am never bashful asking a prurient favor as sometime he is in the mood and sometimes I, we have to be that close. Day and night he is with me even in my dreams. That's what I desire from him."

"No one realizes how strong your love is until you divulge to the person either side. *Kids and wife both wish the head of the family to spend some time with them. Sit with them, Chat with them and hug them, is an emotional energy for them. This is like mental food to keep a dream alive for the next few days. Some houses I have seen, they are economically poor, but emotionally rich. It's entirely because they spend time whenever possible sharing opinions and jokes, solving kids' homework, eat and work together. These bonds together closely. Children are more open to share."* Shankar explained

"But sir, my hubby owns a travel job, can't remain for more than 7-8 days a month. I feel alone without him sometimes desperate without his feel. Does this mean I shouldn't have married him" A lady stated

"Yes you are true, but we need to understand, does he feel the same? Yet he works, all for keeping home alive. In such situation either he stops the business or you sacrifice as long as he is doing for you and a home. You look educated, learn some profession and proceed. You need to keep yourself busy to avoid negativity dominating you. All worldly ecstatic are temporal, may one day coax you to regret. In your life good and rough, negative and positive, joy and sorrow go along with you, you have to live with and endure to be loyal to the individual who is loyal to you. I have already explained 'learn to live with what you have'." Shankar said

"Without a companion, lonely life hurts and is painful, we curse why were we born? With companion we have all physical and mental events to share. Now I realize how important my wife was for me" Prem said painfully.

"Loneliness is a way of life for me" dispirited Darshan perorated "I still feel her in my dreams. She comes and solaces me in my loneliness."

"Yes, loneliness is cruel punishment. No-one shares your feelings. Yet it is better than living with heartless kids." Saleem said

"Just assume you came alone and will go alone. They are only the resources for your karma, will accompany you as long as their karma attached to you. When is over they leave. The deeper the attachment the greater the pain while departing, establishes the sincerity in love and closeness. Meditate to cool yourself from inside; you will feel Godly feelings inside you." Simon said

Darshan looked at Saleem and recited a poem of '**anathema of an aging man**':

I am Aged of eighty,
Have no, no convive,
No partner of life,
who pays attention to,
the narrative I have;
We aged need not much,
but good memories,
And a glimpse of kids,
To live the rest of life;
I am a deserted aged man,
Searching for something,
Fills my lonesome life;
Sitting in chair outside my bungalow,

Of 4 luxury rooms and 5 maids,
Surrounded by virgin mountains;
All greenery exhilarating view,
fluttering cool dancing lake,
making vibrant teasing sound;
birds sitting on a tree,
too tweet teasing song,
'O' lonely lovelorn man,
This world isn't fit for you,
good for couple who love to chat,
We watch you sit all alone,
watching us we sing,
Enjoy in pair;
Cool breeze too ruffles,
Says "you lonely piece of barren terra,
Find someone to moist your soul,
Dampen your soul to feel,
Ecstatic chilly breeze;
Find someone,
Warm your chill;
it's a heaven meant for pair";
can't enjoy nature's features,
unless you are contended man;
promising thought blew my mind,
I have no one sharing thoughts,
In my old age I have no one to live for,
Not even kids,
they send greetings full of stupid quotes,
And say thank you papa,
you are inspiration for life;
In all occasions receive
junk greeting mail and cards,
Dump them in bin;
I lived for wife and for kids,
Did not remarry was mistake;
life is Sahara totally dry,
In this age no one wants;
How long bear old age curse,
Many in this age,
Suffer grieved life worst than I;
they abandon aged,

Live and let live

dump in old age home;
and send the greetings,
inflicting pain already injured;
World is mean live or not,
No one cares;
Greeting cards are no worth for us,
You stupids don't know!
Aged only need someone listen,
the story they have;
we are aged need no much,
but good memories and,
a glimpse of kids to live rest of life......

Mostly all aged and middle aged agreed with the poem. One mushy aged man, tears in eyes emotively said "is true, *we want nothing, take all from us what we have. But share some time and listen to what we have. We don't live to hurt you, but need a bit of care and a feel of recourse.*"

An aged of 90 supported by his son, said his words "*We also lived through the age you have. We too were tied and gave birth to kids like you. Mother and Father had their position, we could never dare challenge in our time. They had respect, and we had respect. Please don't neglect us; we make mistakes, forgive us as do with your kids*"

Driven by the disconsolate situation of aging people, Shankar gestured all four Saleem, Darshan, Prem and Simon "as a part of Karma yoga, we will visit all the homes in our neighborhood, you need to actively participate. I too will contribute towards redressing domestic crisis."

Judge and the advocate too, took initiative "if you agree, we will get our league registered to legalize and with the help of police stations, NGO's, local hospitals we shall achieve the objective."

"That's true, even aged dry leaves shall show their worth to the society. Thanks to your valuable idea" the aged woman commented

Chitra, Aabidah, Neelam, and Anne from young batch, the middle aged women Paramjeet, Azra, Ana too offered for dynamic membership. One said "though we can't eradicate completely yet can guide to sanctify to live happy life"

The advocate asked "please come forth and give your names. For aged and the women's issues we shall have registered as recognized association. Our responsibility will be visiting each and every house and assuage the situation occurrences to support the victims."

"We need to create awareness among home members, not by strength but by spiritual awakening. We will continue yoga each day sharp at 5. And then social awareness, debate" Shankar urged

Shankar found people's faces feeble and sad due to irksome discussions. He once again sat on the ground folding both legs together on each. Asked all to perform the way he did, and then directed "please shut your eyes easefully. Continue searching in mind for the funniest or touching memory of your life until you get. Remain still for some time and rapt in best, funniest part of the past. The neurotransmitters dopamine, endorphins and serotonin chemicals are all released to enchant your body, mind and soul, appear on your face and cheek. You are happy with smile on your face for the moment. You create exhilarating surroundings so others enjoy your company. The face will glow; the sheen will overwhelm your look."

Waited to watch the smiles in most persons and said again "After office hours when you reach home, please perform this and see the change in your home. A smile comes from sentience signifies your happiness. You will start loving all beings."

"So you mean one need to be capricious and prankish to create funny memories" a lady in the crowd elvishly said

"Yes, true, we don't remember all but the most attractive is always in our memory. The prankish jokes, Romany incidences, cordial friend's memories travel along with us lifelong" Darshan laughed while saying

"*Root cause of all unpleasant happenings in or outside home is because we aren't happy and content. The greed has no limit, extends before you accomplish one. Ego arises from inferiority complex. Anger is a sign of weakness. Fear arises from the guilt and lack one has. Content people are complete and find exigency within their range. They live in philosophy of 'don't look for love here and there when you have one at home'. Each individual is beautiful, some have outer beauty and some hold inside. Accept as is and embellish to feel the gaiety.*" Shankar said

All welcomed the sayings of Shankar "thanks for amicable guidelines of life, will try our best to meet the touchstone"

Shankar after hearing various opinions said "*there are so many domestic issues, but the solution is one word 'contentment'. Contentment thwarts all strategic tools of the fiend. When you have this in your mind, you have everything*" then he joined his palm together, said "Namaskar, will meet at 5 tomorrow."

Next day, Saleem was absent, poetic ambience missing the feel of touch. Birds tweeted gloomy sounds. Dew too felt no more freshness; with no poem we are dry. Falling petals said there is something wrong. Sun though rose was glum, expecting melodic strings.

Darshan asked friends "where is Saleem. Without him it is dry"

"Isn't here, may be busy, will check after this" Prem said comforting Darshan, and then concentrated to hear the discourse.

Shankar prepared himself for the Yoga. He sat straight folding his legs over each knee. "Namaskar, first we finish with the rest of the postures of Kundalini

Yoga." Waited for a moment to judge people and said "I know there may be Muslims, Christians, Hindus, Sikhs, Jewish here in this meet. 'OM' is a verbal exercise that creates vibration within to energize. 'AUM' or 'OM' is a universal word, has no religion, good for all, and was discovered during the Vedic age much-much before the rise of all the regions."

He closed his eyes to focus and asked to pronounce with him 'OM'. Stretch each letter like 'oooooo' then 'mmmmmm'. And repeat as I do. Both your mouth and nose function together during the chant. You feel stretching belly, pulsating heart, speeding veins in the brain and lungs while sound releasing into the air. Our mind, aura, nose, ear is the third sensory tools without revealing us function to explore surroundings. That is the cause we sometimes feel the presence unnoticed by the eyes. Daily chanting of 'OM' strengthens your senses. It is an exercise to activate functions of sensory."

For some respite, he waited and began "take deep breath, hold for some time to your ability and slowly release." All followed the way Shankar wished.

Then Shankar directed "now we are prepared to perform 'stretch pose'. Stretch your legs straight as we performed yesterday lay your arms straight down by your sides. Stretch the spine of your cervix. Lift upper chest, head and arms off the ground and pull your chin in. Point your fingers and stare at your toes. Keep your lower back flat against the ground as you lift the legs slightly off the ground, toes pointed. If your lower back stresses you, keep the heels lightly resting on the ground or put your hands underneath your sacrum, hold for 2-3 minutes. First inhale by relaxing the upper abdominal muscles, allowing air to fill the lungs. Then exhale by quickly pulling the navel point and solar plexus in and upwards toward the backbone as you push the breath away. Take even inhales and exhales to 2 to 3 cycles per second."

After doing all six exercises Shankar said "we relax for a while and begin the social issue. The purpose of all the Yoga exercises is to cool soul, mind, and body and finally achieve the 'contentment'. The contentment is the way of life for compassion, forgiveness, caress, endearment, and loyalty to spirituality and finally it is *live and let live*"

"Yeah, it's the time for social insight" A man from the crowd said.

"Each one has a problem in this world as a result of undue craving. Sometimes things don't come to your expectation stresses you, results exertion. Sometimes your craving is beyond your competence, agitates you, incur efforts assertively to achieve is also a form of disruptisfaction, when fail frustrates you. Therefore, the positivity is to do your best and if failure accept with cheer. Halt for some time and attempt again and again calmly. Failure is not you lost all, rather, is a lesson to correct deficiency before climbing next step of the ladder. Content with what you have is the philosophy of life for happiness." Shankar explained

An aged woman accompanied by her daughter in law, came with the issue "I and my daughter in law with her children live together without any conflict. She is 62 and I am 87. We both worked in small private companies for over 25 years with meager wage. Now we have no income or pension, surviving in old age life is miserable. We both are patients without proper medication. In our good age, we worked hard but could not save money enough. Why Government's can't consider our old age plight. Are we less humans than the others."

Simon agreeing the point stated "This is a serious issue, over 70% of world over suffer. No free or subsidized medication, no pension scheme for informal sector workers, no proper old age homes and hospitals. It is a human rights issue; we should all fight for it."

"This issue needs national and the international attention through Non Government Organizations or any affiliated bodies. However, we have applied for registration of our league so can move without hurdle." Judge said

A disgruntled man in the crowd waited his chance to talk out his torture as a doer in the informal sector "I am a worker in a large shop in Chandni Chowk. I have been working for 40 years without any privilege. Today I am 58 years old with no intensity as in younger years. Off and on getting scolded and bluster of getting fired. The future is dark, where will I go, what I will make out in my old age without social protection and pension" he bent his head in sorrow.

"A large percentage of the work force employed in the unorganized sector without any privilege of human consideration. Though is sensitive predicament, yet I feel as complicated task for the Government to bring self employed and hired by others together to consider pension scheme." The advocate made his view point

A sociology student couldn't hold patience, retorted "where there is a will there is a way out. Each living person is human and deserves to survive like human. Governments and the International bodies are responsible to treat this issue as human rights. If the Government is serious without joking with people can take on the same pension scheme as formal sectors by slight fluctuations.

- Social security/Aadhar card is enough to register the informal workers. The card number may be treated as the depository financial institution account number. The generated account number is fed electronically on the card.

- Make mandatory the specified amount deposited by the beneficiary each month/year minimum in the Post office or the nearest banks.

- For self employed, Aadhar card registration number be made mandatory, that can as well be used as license to run his show. Routinely scrutinize his contribution on the spot by electronic machine or tab.

- Add Government contribution whatever towards social security to below poverty line or in the edge of the poverty line. In case of employees, affordable contribution of employers added to the Government minimum contribution.

- For informal sector employees, medical scheme be introduced for the old age or 15 years after the contribution.

- Each block village or municipal to have a mini hospitals or mobile hospitals to care aged people.

This is an acute problem needs attention of the state and central Government as over 90% of the work force is in unorganized sectors in South Asian countries.

The advocate reminded the incidence of an aged woman who was pushed out of house "We have prepared legal notices to two curators of aged lady and man we met last day will be served in two days. Let us see what we can do better for them."

Within a month the court notice was served to the lady to appear before the court. The aged lady's right to home was restored. In addition served ruling of rupees 5000 as maintenance allowance by daughter in law. Judge also authorized victim to levy rent for the occupancy. The judge in his verdict announced jail for 3 months for harassing aged lady. Also had advised a few points to the Government:

- To open up old age homes in all hospitals with free medical care in order to help poor aged over 75.

- Assign local police stations and local municipal to visit regularly and register the names. Follow up regularly for safety.

- For aged over 75, Post offices and Banks render free home service.

- Introduce a pension scheme and free medical care for their old age, who serves in informal sectors. They are also as humans as employees of organized sectors.

- Arrange mobile medical care units for aged. We are humans so humanity is our first priority.

- Let this be a lesson to all ageing people that will not gift their property to children as long as they are alive. Even if they want, they give 'will' eligible after death.

The discussion, informal sector as such was critical; the Judge Iyyer waited his turn to say "The active members I think are ready to accompany us to start visiting from today."

All said in one voice "we are prepared"

"We will meet together at 7pm and start follow. But as today is Sunday we can start right now" Judge said

Darshan suggested "may I request you to consider first visit to Saleem's home. He is an unwanted man for his children."

Judge and the Advocate led the team of 12 to Saleem's house knocked the door, but no response. Nevertheless, after 3 knocks, the door was opened, went straight to Saleem's bed pitiably laid in the open unclean courtyard. Pitcher with water in and a plate for food placed under the bedside.

Darshan got wild, but Judge politely patted his shoulder and asked "be patient, we will take care"

Judge called his son "come hither, we need to talk to you"

Son enquired "Who are you? In what capacity have you forcefully entered into my house?"

"I am a judge" gestured his right, "he is an advocate" and pointed on his left "she is a human rights activist". The Judge said

Son embarrassed looked at all "I will call police"

Judge ignored him "What relationship do you have with him?"

"He is my father"

Judge looked at his face piteously and said "are you not ashamed?"

"I am not the only son, there are two more. Why can't he stay with them?"

Darshan in the meantime chatting with Saleem watched his face had finger marks "what is this?"

"Son slapped me and his wife accompanied him by kicking me" Saleem sobbed violently

"Why"

Unable to hold his weep, said "They want to kick me out of the house," he hissed in pain "still pains"

Judge too came to see the marks and said to the son "You are a criminal. Will pay for this" without wasting time he took his mobile out of pocket and called the police station "I am a high court judge and I want senior most person immediately report" he explained the address to reach.

Advocate asked other team members "not to let these criminals escape. Hold them."

Prem's emotion was at the height phoned a woman "Where are you?"

"I am at home" the woman answered

Prem asked "A Hot news for you. Can you please come and take video?"

"Ok" She without wasting time rushed to the place.

Within a short time the inspector reached in his jeep. Saluted the judge and said "Deputy Commissioner is on his way" Inspector took a note to frame a charge. Then, on the complaint letter took Saleem's signature.

"We are taking Saleem to the hospital for medical reports and care. The report we will use as an evidence of criminal activity" the inspector said.

The humiliated son and his wife, knelt before the judge, said in hissing sound "Won't repeat again, please excuse us." The woman touching his feet repeatedly said "Won't repeat. Sorry for this shameless act. Please... please don't punish, will shatter us. Our kids will go forlorn"

Ignoring them asked lady police to repel them and asked the assistant commissioner "give the copy of the report"

"OK, sir" and handed over a second copy of the first investigation report.

"Arrest them." Ignoring son and his wife's pleading the judge directed police.

A woman already taking video of all incidences said "I will have this cruelty telecast in the TV channel"

Saleem was too infirm to walk sought help of Prem and Darshan. While going to the hospital, he said "I don't want to stay with them anymore"

"I am alone in my three storeys home. I will love your company" Darshan said

The following day after the yoga session the Judge, Advocate, Darshan, Simon and Prem visited Saleem in the hospital. Simon after inquiring his health condition got to the doctor's room and demanded the condition.

Doctor replied "there is nothing to worry, but may take a week to recover the knee injury." They together went to Saleem's bed

"How do you feel?" Doctor said

"Bit relief" Saleem said

"There is nothing to panic. He is alright" the doctor assured

After a few chats all departed saying "will visit in the evening" Prem, Darshan, Prem and Simon stayed back

Simon came over to the window to watch the ambiance outside. Partly cloudy, hidden behind black clouds, Sun snooped earth's ruse.

Simon said "intense traffic and smoke released by cars and buses are helping clouds darken. Clouds too headstrong, has in mind 'I am hurt by your misdeed, Will send the same back to you as slush. What you sow, so you reap'"

Meanwhile Darshan asked Prem "Are you not hungry? What happed to our breakfast?"

Prem chafing his belly looked at him "yes... Yes, why not?" He went towards canteen in the ground floor.

Placed an order "4 Dosa, 4 sandwiches, 4 glasses juice and coffee" waited for sometime during preparation. While waiting he sat close to TV news, Saleem's sound drew his attention. It was on TV news, watched carefully. At once he called Ranjana, the TV woman "thanks"

She said "ok. You are great. Don't forget me when you need such help"

"Are you free tomorrow morning" Prem asked

"Yes, why?" Ranjana replied

"Will you be free enough to join our Yoga class" Prem asked

Rajana in loud sound asked her husband "where are you? Can we move together to yoga class?"

"What time?" The husband replied inhibiting his song in the lavatory.

"At 5 am for yoga class"

"No, you go I am busy in bed tomorrow," he said in jesting sound

"Idiot" Ranjana retorted in anger

"Ha... Ha... Ha... Ha..." the husband laughed

Prem heard everything "tell him there is a drinks party at 4am"

"Don't worry for a drink; he is always ready anytime and anywhere. I will be there right at 5am" Ranjana replied

In 20 minutes the breakfast was quick. Prem went and fetched some 4 paper plates and 8 glasses and came through lift to avoid stuff getting cold.

Entered the room and stated "Here it is. Let's start" and began to pour juice and coffee, placed Dosa and sandwiches on separate plates. All started their morning feed.

"For many years I haven't tasted Dosa" Saleem said

Prem while chewing a mouth full sandwich said in a blurry sound unclear to all "TV channel news... bla... Bla"

"Finish in your mouth first and say" Simon said

Prem finished and a sip of coffee to swallow, said "I saw TV news coverage of Saleem's incident. In the news it was more eerie than we physically experienced"

"Thus, no escape to his son" Darshan said

Saleem did not say a word, but the soreness of son's punishment was puzzling him inside. The worry of children and the grandchildren bothered him at heart. Finally caved in his silence and stated "I am concerned about my children. What will happen, I don't know?"

"I understand your pain. However, there is no chance for them to escape the justice. It is now publicly broadcasted" Darshan said

"This should be a lesson for them and others to recognize the consequences" Prem said

"Yes, it is painful when own son gets punishment through father" Simon said while collecting the glasses and the plates to dump into waste box.

Spent some more time before departing and said together "will visit in the evening"

In the evening at 5.30 pm Judge with his friend advocate arrived. I inquired about his health

"I am recovering" Saleem said

"We are missing your poems. Please get well soon. All are gloomy without your vitalizing poems." Judge said with a grin.

The advocate went straight to the doctor's room "how is Saleem?"

"Nothing to worry, He will be freed in 2 days" doctor replied

"Thanks" and arrived back to the room

Saleem gestured with his hand the judge and wished to come nearer to his bedside. Judge went to him, inclined his head closer to Saleem's face.

Saleem whispered in his ears "will court punish my kids hard?"

Bewildered Judge looked at Saleem "It is a grave criminal offense and they will pay for that. Why are you calling for now?"

"Whatever they may have behaved to me, after all, they are my children, and how will I hold up their sufferings" Saleem said

"I understand the father's pain, but now it is also tardy. Moreover, the incidence has been covered by TV channel" the advocate said

"But..." the sourness reflected in his expression. "Will he miss his job?" Saleem asked

"The clemency of elderly, here we lose to our youngsters. Don't be that soft, please" the advocate said

Judge soothed him by caressing his shoulder "Don't worry; entire team of our league is with you. We will do all necessary to protect you"

"I have already filed; a hearing will be any time shortly. The justice will be done" the advocate said

"The justice never takes the side of anyone. Nor does it have eyes or heart. It abides by only one point 'justice', examines the crime before giving any justice" the justice stated

"Let this be an example for others" the advocate said and moved out of the room with the judge saying "get strong." While at the door, they met Azra another middle age widow member of the team and wished each other.

She did and looked at Saleem's face smiling "How are you?"

Saleem nodded "recovering now"

She sat beside him without any conversation for some time. Both were thinking where to commence.

"Thanks for calling me" Saleem said

"Today I came early from the office and prepared Biryaani, brought to you and your allies. Where are they?" She said quietly to him

"They will be here at any time," he stated

"Your allies are as just as your poems" she stated

"Are you living with your kids?" He asked her

"One is in U.S and the other in U.K, all with their families" she stated

"How often they visit you?" He quietly asked

"For the past 4 years never, only sometimes a telephone call" had her face down "being alone is really irritating. Sometimes I feel why I permitted them to settle overseas"

"Luckily, your children are not with you, else your luck would have been same as mine. Sort of more control on you." Saleem said

Darshan, Prem and his daughter in law Neelam, and Simon entered. They wished Azra.

Neelam asked "when did you come?"

"Just half an hour back" Azra said

Neelam looked at her face with a smile "you look well today"

She removed large Tiffin carrier from her bag and said "dinner for you all is here". And she got up to go.

"I will company you to ground floor" Neelam said

"Ok"

Azra moved towards lift, but Neelam pulled her hand "no, we go walking"

On the way Neelam looked at her face and smiled, without holding anything inside "do you love him?"

Azra was amazed hearing, only recognized it as her turning point said "yes" and succumbed in shyness.

"Did you propose?" Neelam asked

"I am a woman, how you expect me to propose?" Ezra then said

"Any gesture" Neelam asked

"Not in the clearest sense, however I feel embarrassed proposing him" Azra said

"May I work as mediator" Neelam asked

Azra did not say anything but smiled and looked Neelam in girlish style.

"It means I should start from today" Neelam said pinching her face

Neelam came back to the room looking at all. Were busy gossiping and then looked at Prem and smiled

Prem asked "where were you?"

"I went to see her off" Neelam said

"Very late, Biryaani is waiting for you," Simon said

Simon opened the box. Neelam took a spoon and started putting on plates. The flavor of spices was so seductive enticed to lick even fingers. All began the feast.

Neelam said "so tasty, looks she understood the taste of uncle Saleem"

"Shut up" Prem said. But none observed the motive behind her saying except Saleem.

Next day in yoga class the hot topic was the TV telecast and the occurrence with Saleem. Everybody whispered about the brutality and the rescue by the yoga team. One said "thank you very much for your teachings that inspired to act for rescue"

"Yes, true, we were inspirited by the honorable Acharya Shankar's the logic lectures. Thanks sir" the judge said

Prem introduced Ranjana to all, "she is a woman behind the exposure of cruel incidence"

"We all thank her for her endeavor. Thanks" The Advocate said

Darshan, Prem, and Simon hailed in appreciation for his helping nature. "Because of you our friend is safe now. We feel encouraged"

Shankar said "now it is time for the purpose we all have gathered" Commenced explaining "today I give an example of Saleem's consciousness of forgiveness and compassion. We all have watched the brutal act of his son on him. The physical pain and the mental torture he endured was no less than surviving the hell. Nevertheless, the cruelty could not instigate him for revenge. Instead, he sought a wish to forgive the children for their crime. It signifies, the impact of forgiveness is stronger than one hurts"

Shankar paused a while before performing "ok we start now the Matsyasana or in English it is called Fish Asana. Those who have high or low blood pressure may abstain from doing this asana"

"Please follow," he lay flat on his back, legs straight joined together asked "Now your hands relaxed place beneath your hips, palms facing down. Bring your elbows closer together with each other. Breathing in, bring your chest and head upward. Hold your chest high. Breathing in, lift your head and the chest up. Keeping the chest high, lower the head backward and touch the top of the head to the ground. With the head lightly touching the ground, press the elbows firmly into the ground, placing the weight on the elbow and not on the head. Raise your chest up from in-between the shoulder blades. Press the thighs and legs to the primer. Hold the pose for as long as you easily can, taking gentle, long breaths in and out. Relax into the pasture with every exhalation. Now lift the head up, lowering the chest and head to the floor. Bring the hands back on the sides of the body and relax."

A bit of relaxation and then Shankar sat folding his legs over each "now we go for next Ardha Matsendra Asana (half spinal twist). Kneel down with your legs together, resting on your heels. Then sit to the right of your feet. Lift your left leg over your right, placing the foot against the outside of the right knee. Bring your right heel in close to your buttocks. Keep the spine erect. Stretch your arms out to the sides at shoulder level, and twist around to the left. Now bring the right arm down on the outside of the left knee and hold the left foot in the right hand, placing your left hand on the floor behind you. While exhalation, twist as far as possible to the left. Look over the left shoulder. This asana is good for the elasticity of your spine and opens your lungs." Shankar after relaxing a bit now we switch over to our next affair.

The aged lady came forth to say thanks "that day's incidence and the action by the honorable Judge impacted widely in my home. My son and his wife now behave very cordially. A fear among them is the outcome. I thank the media also for widespread exposure."

"Domestics clashes in whatever form, are activated by accumulation of small-small untoward incidences bursts one day. You can resolve easily by sharing and communicating with each other. Things you don't like, say at face, but softly without hurting ego, maybe afterwards, when the flame is quenched. Mind it, no one is perfect all need guidelines for change" Shankar explained

A couple, accompanied by the aged parents, came forth to put their helplessness to Shankar "we have been persuading them for the past one year to live with us in Hampshire" the son said but before he could continue she intercepted and said her version "Look we cannot leave jobs for their sake. We have day boarding too we pick up them as we do with our kids"

The son continued "they are very stubborn to accept our invitation. We can't be in peace by abandoning them in helpless condition. Why don't they realize they will have no help to even make a cup of tea? Even the servants you cannot trust in urban cities"

Father finally broke his silence, said "firstly, I can't adjust with western culture. Secondly, I won't sell my house for the sake of migrating to western world. My house is security to my wife and me. I can't play with this, my son"

Son on that replied "Western too are as humans as we are, may be better than us as they care aged better than us. Don't sell house for us, even if you sell house the money will remain with you"

Son's Wife continued convincing the aged through this platform "They have all the facilities an aged wants. There too isolation and loneliness exist, but they have day boarding system to narrow the gap."

"Dad, I don't compel to sell your house, rent it out to who you trust. Then come with us, me and my children want you and your money." The son said in deep worry. Paused for some time in wet eye to speak again, said "I warn you, we aren't leaving India without you"

"You have better facility and medication and above all good same aged friends. In all means better than India. You will suffer physically without any hearing and we mentally worrying each day and night of your well being "Political foul odor smells in India"

"You too were born in this country" the mother in law said

"Yes, I, you and all of us were born in this country when it was fresh, had not rotten to stink foul smell. People were good, leaders were good and the ambiance was good" the daughter in law said

Listening all Shankar, said *"someone said old age is child age. They are so adapted to living the way they are since their childhood is not easy to transform in the old age. Fear of insecurity in mingling with new ambiance coerces to stay back to own created ambiance. The same situation is also with them. Only consolation, sense of security and trust can change the mentality of the aged. Therefore it is the responsibility of the children to create confidence."*

"There is lot of difference in their and our social behavior. Not easy to adjust there. Long back I had experienced the same" Darshan said

"Without choice they have to adjust in atmosphere where they feel security. The dedicated children are their security" Prem commented

The discussion was ended, both aged couple agreed to stay with the children.

Neelam went to Azra, said "the class is over now. Shall we go to that corner if you are not late to the office?"

Azra said "I have some work pending at the office. Let me check if my coworker can handle and complete," she took her phone out and conversed. It took some time to make her understand. Then she called her boss to seek off from office. "Now I am fully free for a day"

Neelam watched Prem coming to her shouting from far away "are you not coming home?"

"No... It's day for you and your son to cook"

Prem raised his both hands together above his shoulder and said "Ok... Ok...," moved with his son towards the home.

"I have not discussed yet with respected Saleem but gave some clue. However, I want to be sure the depth of love in him for you" Neelam said again "don't take it otherwise, what did you find in him to get attracted"

"He is a poet. Normally poets are cool, but a little bit stubborn. Such people know love. Above all he is 'Muslim' if I articulate in more refined word 'Islam'. In Islam widow can remarry freely, but with Muslims only. Hence I took him." Azra said

They together walked towards Azra's home to prepare breakfast. On the way while walking, Neelam's curiosity to know more about Islam mounted, she asked "what 'Muslim' is and what 'Islam' is?"

"Why are you so curious?" Azra asked

"Because what has been fed in our head is the Muslim means radicalism" Neelam said

"Yes true, they fight for equality, peace, and justice. For us all humans are same irrespective of religion or caste then why there is social and economic inequality." She paused a moment and recited Quran verse "Qur'an 4:135: O ye who believe! Stand out firmly for justice, as witnesses to Allah, even as against yourselves, or your parents, or your kin, and whether it is (against) rich or poor: for Allah can best protect both. Follow not the lusts (of your hearts); lest ye swerve, and if ye distort (justice) or decline to do justice, verily Allah is well-acquainted with all that ye do."

Azra took her keys out to open the door. Opened the door "Welcome home"

Live and let live

Both went straight way to kitchen. Azra opened the fridge and asked "What you wish to eat?"

Neelam replied "Something special of your pick. Today I am with a special woman"

"Ok, we make masala omelet and goat Keema stuffed paratta" Azra checked the availability of curd in the fridge and together began to prepare.

A ring in the mobile of Neelam "it is call from my husband" she replied the call "take keys with you or give to father in law. Today I am with Azra my beautiful sister"

While cooking Azra said "where were we?"

"Muslim and Islam" Neelam said

She continued the meaning of both terms "For that first I have to explain 'Allah'. Perhaps you are aware, our religion started from Arab all terms are used in Arabic word. 'Allah' is also an Arabic word of 'God'. Is it clear?"

"Yes" Neelam said

"Now we come to 'Muslim'. The meaning of Muslim is "the one who submits to 'God', in Arabic term 'Allah'. Surrendering to Allah means compassion, love, equality and purity."

"Then why they go for killing, raping women" Neelam asked

"The real Muslims do not rape women, but protect them; they fight for justice but don't kill innocents. Those who kill or rape are black sheeps, don't stick to Islamic values. Each faction has negative and positive side. In negative atmosphere the negativity arises" Azra said

Neelam while tasting omelet and Paratta "Delicious. You are a good cook"

Azra too, took a pinch of food "good" and opened the fridge, took the curd pot out and lay on the table. Neelam made coffee and asked Azra "if sweetness ok?"

"Ok, good"

While eating Neelam asked "now guide me about Islam?"

"Again an Arabic word "Salema": peace, purity, submission and obedience. In the spiritual sense, Islam means submission to the will of God and obedience to his law. "Inda deena inda lahi Islam." (Certainly, the only acceptable way which Allah will accept is Islam)." Azra said

Azra took a sip of coffee and said again "As a result of repression in the Gulf and Africa, rebellion spread out over to other sections. Unfortunately a major percent of victims were Muslims. Most downtrodden from all the religions would one day voice against repression if the situation remains like this. The rich is so ample that he can't handle his bulky wealth and on the other side is poor who can't even hold one time food. No religion asks for this!"

Live and let live

Neelam grasped from Azra's thoughts "during antiquity in Hindu temples free food and clothing was served to needy poor. Even today in some temples, food distribution exist"

"This is called compassion for the hapless. Even once I went to the Gurudwara, ate blessed dainty" Azra said, taking a spoon full of curd in her mouth.

"You mean unequal distribution of resources and the economic tyranny has ignited the uprise." Neelam commented

"Yes, *'everything belongs to Allah and Allah belongs to all'*. All religious inscriptions guide to equality say for:

Rig: 5-59-6 says "Te ajyesthaa akanisthaasa udbhido amadhyamaaso mahasaa vi vavridhuh | sujaataaso janushaa prishnimataro divo marya aa no achaa jigatana ||" – Rig: 5-59-6 Among these men there are no superiors or no inferiors, no middle ones either. They become great from small beginnings. They make progress in different ways by dint of their merits. By birth they are all highborn because they are all children of Mother-Earth. O you men of the Lord Refulgent! Be available to us in a loveable manner or grow into praise-worthy souls in fairways"

Galatians 3:28 ESV: There is neither Jew nor Greek, there is neither slave nor free, there is no male and female, for you are all one in Christ Jesus."

They finished their snack "We prepare lunch and dinner for Saleem and his allies"

Neelam washed each plate, placed them properly "let me call my father in law" took her mobile to speak "Do you need me there?"

"Are you busy?' Prem asked

"Yes, we are preparing lunch and dinner for Saleem and allies" Neelam said

"Don't play foul to repent later" Prem said

"Don't worry daddy, will organize nicely" Neelam said

"You will be entirely responsible" Prem said

"Please arrive with your friends to hospital at 2pm. Bring the kids along" Neelam said

"Ok" Prem answered and both switched off the telephone sets

Azra and Neelam both got engaged in getting material ready for cooking. Azra took from the fridge the boneless meat, Keema, some green pea, some onions, tomatoes, cheese and some potatoes. Handing over peas, onions, potatoes to Neelam, asked "peal them please"

Neelam placed them on the table, knife in her hand and first started pealing onion. Her eyes got red dropped unemotional itching tears. Her nose got wet took the edging of her sari, wiped her wet nose. In a few minutes she chopped them systematically into nice pieces, asked "Is the size ok"

"Yes... Yes perfect" Azra said while bringing flavored Basmati rice to clean.

Neelam took rice from Azra's hand, cleaned "the flavor of the rice is very aromatic"

In the meantime Azra went toward the corner of the kitchen cabin to get some cardamom, cashew nuts, dry grapes, cloves, sliced almond, saffron, and some spices "today we prepare Keema curry, meat Biryaani, cheese-peas with some potato curry, and some Keema stuffed parattas."

Neelam lit the stove and pan on it. In a hot pan she poured some cow cream, added sliced onions with some spices. She waited until the ingredients got enough reddish. While Stirring ingredients for equal fry, she stated "Now should I put Keema"

"Yes" Azra said while frying cheese on another burner. After turning a bit brownish added spices, then removed from the pan to another plate, added sliced onion, salt, turmeric, coriander powder, and some black pepper powder, waited until got brownish. Added peas and potatoes into it by adding some water and left to seethe.

"Sometimes my father in law, when he is alone lost in a different universe. I have seen even weeping sometimes. Literally, I saw tears in his eyes. Makes me worry" Neelam said while stirring after adding some more salt into cooked Keema curry. Got hold of a teaspoon full curry to Azra "taste it and say"

"Ok" Azra said while taking out the lid to check cheese pea curry condition. She again asked "How is your and son's rapport with him"

"He is my deepest friend. He is a better father than my own. I like him more than my hubby. He is really cool and cordial" Neelam said while pouring milk into pan then boiled twice to harden before putting some white rice to prepare Kheer (desert).

Neelam said again "his mental agony worries me. I never want to see him in pain. He drinks at night, accompanied my husband and the gossip till midnight. Hence at least he has sound sleep and forgets all. Sometimes I accompany them, but no whisky"

"I don't propose this" Azra said

"I guess because you are Muslim" Neelam said

Without replying to Neelam, Azra got busy with pealing cardamom. Crushed seeds to powder then took a pan and placed on the stove to fry dry fruits "We will use saffron in later stage"

"I believe he is missing his wife. They would have had a good wave length. When did she die?" Azra asked during segregating coriander leaves

"I think five years. Yes, since then he moans but never brings out the pain deep down him. Many nights he walks round the balcony without sleep." Neelam said while stirring milk. Took a bit of rice to check if was cooked well "It still needs and bit of boiling. Should I pour more milk?"

Azra went to her to check if more milk needed "how many are we?" She began counting with fingers. Prem, Saleem, Simon, Darshan, your two kids and us both "Yes we need more milk"

"Ok" Neelam did the same and waited till it boiled then added sugar stirred for some time with a tablespoon. Took a teaspoon full of Keeer (desert) to taste. "It's very sweet now; my father in law can't eat"

"Is he diabetic?" Azra asked

"Yes" Neelam replied

"We remove the pan, use for cooking the meat" Azra asked.

Azra placed pan on the stove and meat on it. Poured some cow cream to fry, stirred till turned brown. "Did he ever tell you about his wife?"

"Never, but my husband always repeats. I want and try to be like her." Neelam said while adding water and rice in rice cooker and switched on the hype.

"He is really lonely, but never lets that appear along his face, does not mean he is glad. How old is he? " Azra said

"He is 63" Neelam said

"Not enough age to be alone. He needs some companion to share his body, mind and emotions, those he can't share with his children" Azra said then she got cooker ready, pouring water in it and put meat into it to boil" Azra said

Neelam thought in her mind, whispered while empting rice from the cooker and put in large pan "something I have to do for his loneliness. He needs some partner"

"What are you whispering" Azra asked while opening lid to check. She took one piece out to stifle "I think now well cooked"

"Not serious, thinking about the loneliness" Neelam said

Azra placed the meat in another bowl. She took some boneless pieces in one bowl. Crushed them and said "left over water of meat we shall make soup" added cloves, chili powder, salt and some vinegar, and let it boil again.

"How you feel about a past husband?" Neelam asked

"So... So... as he had 2 more wives. A woman never likes her love shared by others. Weekly three days he stayed with me, was a celebration for me. He was very caring, loved me, and cared me whenever he was with me. Only grudge between him and me was sharing his love with others. Nevertheless, during 3 days he filled his love in me so much that his absence never troubled me until he died." Azra said, giving in to her past memories "yes I loved him very much"

"Do you feel lonely" Neelam asked

"Tortures me, many sleepless nights I endure" Azra said. She took one piece of meat again to check if done "yes done, we mix meat and hot rice together" Azra said then took a bottle of saffron, cashew nuts, dry grapes, almond cut pieces. Mixed them before covering the lid. "It's ready now"

Azra opened the soup lid and sniffed "I think it is ok now. Let me check again" took in a teaspoon, tasted and added some tomato and chilly soup "now it is ready."

Neelam took some tomatoes, cucumber, onions, banana and apples. Sliced them nicely. Put some pepper, salt and Chaat masala "salad is ready"

"You know; living together, sharing your body and emotions for long with companion, you are totally bonded. Most powerful glue impossible to detach. Emotions overpower you, absence tortures when he is detached. However, the companion who adheres to connection and when is away for some time, the time gap stimulates to decorate yourself to meet his wanting. Retains you busy, you don't feel lonely. He is still in you, in your imaginations and dreams." Azra said while checking the food preparation. "I think we are done. Only to place them into carriers and flask"

"Yes, sometimes I too feel when my husband is away for weeks for office work. None can accommodate. I realize now my father in law's pain" Neelam said

"However, if there is any blemish in the sincerity of both, it means the objective is quenching crave and both are cheaters. *Love does not arise from craving as is devotion and sacrifice*" Azra said while packing them together in the carry bag

Azra waited for a moment for her rising thoughts "do you think he will accept me?"

"There is one hitch that he has no money, no assets and no pension. Will you accept him as is?" Neelam asked

"I loved him and his poems and nothing else, I need from him" Azra said

"Now you leave this to me. I will manage" Neelam said then held one bag "I like you so much and you taught me so much" Neelam hugged her tightening, both her arms covering Azra's back and kissed her both cheeks.

Neelam called for a tuk-tuk scooter rickshaw. When it arrived Azra looked for keys and together carried both bags. Azra locked the door and moved in a rickshaw to hospital.

"Don't you feel shy while contacting Saleem" Neelam whispered in Azra's ears.

"Yes, many times my thoughts pushed me back, but finally I failed and crouched to this lean fellow for his charming poems and smile. Above all the desperation to have someone nice person to live with who cares, strews savor of love, takes me on his chest, kisses me, prettifies my body. Though I am aged over 50 yet if my man if adorns my body, my soul fulfills me" she spoke quietly so only Neelam could hear.

"I am not a widow; still I feel the agony when he does not embrace my body. Sexual desire and relief is so powerful for intimacy" Neelam whispered in her ears

"Yes, true, we exist because of this" Azra said quietly again "for the past 3 years I am mad looking for sensual partner, but somehow I managed by reading the Quran to cool down my craving"

"We are humans like other species, but the social order differentiates us from them" Neelam said in her ears

The tuk-tuk stopped at the hospital. Neelam only paid what was on the meter. Tuk-tuk man objected and began arguing. She took her mobile out and noted rickshaw number. The rickshaw man escaped without giving any clue. They went to the lift and pressed number 3 and reached Saleem's room. A full team of allies were sitting and waiting.

"Ah… finally lunch has arrived" Darshan said

Prem before reaching hospital explained the intention of Neelam. All had agreement to save Saleem from cruel children and loneliness.

Azra took both Neelam's children hugged them and gave them sweet kisses "you have lovely children"

Neelam and Azra together placed bowls with spoons and poured soup. All took their bowls and started sipping. Simon sipped "very hot chili"

Totally enjoyed and sipped soup, after finishing, Neelam and Azra served the second round main course, parattas, cheese pea, Keema curry and some salad.

"One of the best Muslim foods I have ever eaten" Saleem grabbed a spoon and grabbed Keema curry to his mouth "Azra's preparation is marvelous"

Neelam grabbed Prem's hand and took to the door side "should I start right now"

"Yes, but for God sake, don't spoil" Prem asked

"Don't worry, they both like each other and we are only going to link them together" and then Neelam and Prem began coming to join. But Neelam remembered one point, "Can you ask her to fetch a bottle of water after a while? So we have enough time to seek Saleem's opinion"

"Ok" Prem nodded

Meantime Azra observed children felt the heat of spices. She took two small bowls filled desert into them. Took both to lap and began feeding "How you like" both kids smiled, showing all teeth out and looked at her. Azra was ready with spoon filled to feed one by one.

Prem drank bottle full of water and requested Azra "Can you kindly fetch a bottle of water from the canteen?"

Azra understood the motive behind sending her away "Ok" then moved towards the lift to canteen.

In her absence Prem took advantage and asked "Why don't you propose her?"

"What do I have to propose her? I haven't money, home or anything. What kind of comfort am I going to give?"

Prem looked at Neelam's face. She was ready to discuss with Saleem "I have already spoken to her and reached the agreement, she wants nothing except you and sometimes your love poems"

All began laughing "ha... ha... ha... ha..."

"I am fed up of my life and will live with anyone except my own children" a moment later Saleem again whispered lamenting "living with children is slavery"

Neelam got little upset "don't weigh everyone in one scale"

"I know your and Prem's affection, it is exceptional. May Allah bring fortune to your family" Saleem said with remorse

"She may come any time. Be prepared to propose her the moment she comes to the room" Neelam said

Saleem sat straight laughing "ha... ha...Ha... went to the bathroom to wash face and comb hair "how do I look now" back to bed shaping face romantically.

Azra entered the room and placed the bottle on a table looking at Saleem.

"A poem for Azra now comes from my mind. Here it is:

I am an aged dusky man,
Like a bottle of Bordeaux wine,
The older am I,
The Stronger my tipsiness,
I am packed in old Jeroboam bottle;
May be in old filthy bottle,
Yet soul is fresh vigorous,
Inebriating wine;
My soul is prisoner under cork,
Once is released,
gravity is at height;
Squirt my moist aroma,
Exhilarates all for fun;
My body may break or perish,
Even may leave me helpless,
Yet am Bordeaux wine, loved by all,
They all know, more the older am I,
More the tipsiness I have;
I am an aged dusky man,
Like a bottle of Bordeaux wine;

She bent her head in shy smiled "Subhan Allah." But Neelam stared at Saleem's eyes.

Saleem observed Neelam's staring eyes "What? Don't you like the poem" Saleem asked

Neelam came closer and said in his ear, "you have to propose and this is no time for vitality poem"

Everybody looked at Neelam strangely, perhaps did not like her conversation with Saleem. Darshan asked "what's wrong?"

Saleem said "Nothing so serious" looking at Azra Saleem said "A surprising fortune to miserable man has amazed me. Is this dream of heavenly life or real? I'm a lean poor man with no money in hand, even kids victimize me and say go out of their house. No one likes to accommodate me except the allies I have. I am no one in on this land. Scares me when I see a dark side of the future. I know my helpless dark future, you will brighten. But my concern is how my accompaniment will bring light in your life" The tears in the eyes from his drooped face made the ambiance wet emotional. Azra and Neelam too sentimentally stooped their head. Some drops in Azra's eyes and some in Neelam have verified the truth of willingness.

Azra said silently in Neelam's ears, "he is so honest, the truth flows from his mouth"

All looked at Azra expecting her understanding "I am a Government employee is secured till I retire. Want to live with a man who is Muslim and soft at heart, cares me, shares his love. I want no more…" She said softly

Saleem asked Azra to come close and held her both hands "Will you be life partner till I or you die. I promise you my all love only to you. Will care you so much so would sweeten the life of both of us."

Saleem looked at Neelam's face and said "Can I now recite the poem?"

"Why not? This is an auspicious moment we all want to enjoy"

Saleem said my poem is "**Quest of mate, to fill lonely life**"

Sun is dreary if no gleam in it;
The cloud is wretched,
If no rain in it;
Tarn with no aquatic,
Is waste as filthy lap;
I am arid desert,
Fill your moist nectar;
The blaze of solitude,
Burns me alive,
Painful, no one by my side;
Come soak me,
Into your flowing potion,
Quench the dryness;

Feel lonely all my life;
I kneel, take your hand,
Kiss it, embellish it,
And ask will you love me,
Live with me all my life;
I love you as bees for buds,
Follow as shadow all my life;
You are earth I as clouds,
Sprinkle elixir from my soul,
Cool your heart and soul;
Beam of sunlight,
Light up your soul,
Sheen your face, Glow your heart;
Will bring bliss to life,
We two lone won't be alone;

Azra sat back on her knee on the floor and bowed her head down in praying form, whispered saying thanks to Allah "al-hamdulillah... You have saved me" Completed her pray before collecting bowls and spoons from the table, washed them in bathroom. The waste she filled in the polybag to dump in waste box.

Neelam poured desert into the bowls and Azra while serving desert in bowls recited verse from Chapter 30, Verse 21 (sūrat l-rūm) "And among His signs is this that He created for you mates from among yourselves, that ye may dwell in tranquillity with them, and He has put love and mercy between your hearts; verily in that are signs for those who reflect."

Prem said thanks for the treat "we all love your food."

"I thank you all, especially Neelam. I will never forget this moment" Azra said

"Never mind... Give treats always, whenever we are at your home" Darshan said in his gracious voice

Azra smiled bowing her head, said "always welcome"

Darshan, Prem, and Simon sought permission from Saleem and Azra to depart. "Will meet you in the evening, roughly at around 6pm" Darshan came closer to Saleem, said dabbing his shoulder

"Are you not coming?" Prem asked Neelam

"I will come in one hour" Neelam replied

Prem asked Neelam to come closer and said quietly "Ok. But don't delay, they may have to discuss alone."

"I understand" Neelam replied

A few moments later the doctor reached in his round "how are you Saleem?" He checked the wounds and blood pressure "Oh! Normal. You can go tomorrow. Good wishes" Doctor went to another room for checkup

Saleem was happy, but the hitch was where to go?

"The old age tortures when you don't have anything. In young age all my efforts were upbringing children," said with remorse his submission to home and children "I regret I couldn't build a home" Saleem said

"Allah is for all who don't have anyone. Don't repent for what you did. You did your duties towards your family. If they don't follow Allah's command they pay for it and rather they should pay." Azra quoted

"Did you check with your children for Nikaah" Saleem asked

"Yes, I talked to my kids. First, they chose to elude saying in old age, no good. But I gave them no room for their excuses and explained my loneliness. And finally I made them recline." Azra said

"Will they be upset?" Saleem asked

"Let them be. I don't care. When they aren't there to care me, why should I?" Azra said

"Children forget the root of their upbringing when they are married. Most sons are not wrong but are helpless before their wives" Saleem said in deploring state.

"Yes, true, where has our Indian culture lost? Azra said

"However, all depends on how the relationship you had when daughters in law was in her younger age. Most of the time it is the revenge of daughters in law in their old age." Neelam replied while moving to door "will meet you tomorrow"

"How about dinner?" She exclaimed

"Don't worry" Neelam replied

"Ok" Azra commented

Azra somewhat agreed to Neelam's point "we don't see the aftermath effect of the wildness. Daughter in law develops the hateful attitude against the 'in laws' the day she begins undergoing tyranny. May be I did some mistakes becoming an obstruction to their advanced thinking."

"My wife also had a bad relationship with the daughter in law. She hates me because I did not interfere to calm the situation, that she still considered I supported her."

"Nevertheless, this is not the way to punish aged" Azra said lamenting

"Perhaps, daughters in law don't intend to punish but to escape unpleasant atmosphere." Saleem said

"Yes by now they have set up their own world, my presence they may consider as thorn in their flesh" Azra agreed and went outside saying "I will come at 5 with tea and cookies."

Saleem in exultation went towards the mirror in bathroom. Saw his unshaved face, eyes and mouths. He was joyous as achieved the aim of life and 'someone to live for'. Got back to bed dancing and whispering song of Sree 420. Lay flat in the bed dreaming paradise angels hovering over blessing him to ask for boon. Little by little he fell in a deep sleep into real dreams of heavenly life.

Sharp at 5 pm Azra knocked the door but Saleem didn't wake. She entered without disturbing his sleep and waited until he woke up.

"Hey when did you come? I was in good dreams." Saleem said

"Just now" Azra said while pouring tea into a cup and handed over to Saleem with the cookie "I have brought a full jug so if even your allies drop in they too may taste spice tea" then she poured for herself.

While drinking tea she said "will you contact the maulvi for our nikaah tomorrow?"

"Ok, after I am relieved from the hospital" Saleem said

"Knock… Knock at the door" the advocate entered the room and asked Saleem "how are you?"

"Fine, we are planning for Nikaah. Is there any hurdle? I am asking you this as you too are a Muslim." Saleem said

"Just wait for sometime, your case is in the court" advocate said

"What connection does marriage have with the judgment" Saleem asked

"There is, I won't tell you now." Advocate said

"Can we live together?" Saleem asked

"Yes but not in the eyes of the world as she is an earning member. I don't want to give any chance for defeat" advocate said

"How long will the judgment take time" Saleem asked

"May be 10-15 days or maximum one month" advocate replied

Azra poured spice tea with cookies and served to advocate "I never knew you were a Muslim"

"My name is Kaliq; my mother is Muslim and Father Hindu. So I am half Muslim and half Hindu. Same is with my children their mother is Christian and Father is Muslim Hindu" Advocate explained.

Took last sip of tea from the cup and gestured for more "My home is blend of religions as your spiced tea. Tastes good"

Azra poured more tea "I think you like it"

Kaliq took a sip "Yes it's lovely; for me love and compassion is more important than any culture and religion as all are for creation of humanity. Religion has no space if humanity fails" Kaliq said

"You are right, but without religion, we humans are inhuman" Azra said

"For me, religion is a passage to link with Allah, God, Ishwar, and Hashem. No-one has seen yet, but all have experienced Allah, which rises from the soul. My policy is to follow religious inscriptions and become nice man. This is what I have learnt from the religion" Advocate Kaliq explained.

"Subhaan Allah, deep articulation" Saleem said in appreciation

Kaliq was about to ask permission to leave, he found all his allies arrived at the door.

"Finally we have joined" Darshan said while laughing

"Did you ask? What Doctor says? Prem asked

"We can go tomorrow" Azra said

"My home is ready waiting for you" Darshan said while patting Saleem's shoulder.

"Our group got registered under the Societies Registration Act, 1860. We can authentically endeavour to achieve objective" Kaliq announced in happy mood

"Can we live together?" Saleem asked Kaliq

"But not without Nikaah" not before Nikaah

"Be careful, your case is strong, but their lawyer may weaken the scene if you start staying together with an earning wife, though she isn't liable to bear your expenses. Don't give any room to lose maintenance allowance from all your children, under senior citizen Act 2007" Darshan cautioned by saying

"I don't think living together with an earning wife can have any reverse effect, as she may or may not share her earnings. Above all, living together is to reduce stress being alone." Prem replied

"Why to take a chance?" Simon remarked

"Stay with me as long as you wish" Darshan said delightfully

"We will not conceal anything before the court. Judge may consider your loneliness into account. I know law protects aged people" Kaliq said looking at both gloomy faces.

"Shukriya" Saleem thanked

"I will get in touch with the tribunal and try to expedite the proceedings" Kaliq said

Azra looked at her watch and said "it's already half past seven" she began arranging plates and glasses on the table "feast is waiting for us"

"For me no, if don't eat with my wife will vex" Kaliq said

"Share something with us and then with your wife" Saleem appealed

"Ok, very less" Kaliq agreed

While taking full spoon of keema into mouth Darshan said "Luckily we have senior citizen act to protect all of us. But majority of us don't know we too are privileged citizens"

Prem picked rice and a piece of meat in a spoon "Saleem you are lucky to have company of a good cook"

Kaliq consented "is real nice food" took handful of Biryaani in his mouth and pronounced in the unclear voice while chewing "you know! When you have someone best food maker is always remembered. Reveals how much one gives care to your taste"

"Biryaani is very yummy" remembering past day of visit Simon said "two days back we had visited an aged couple of age 70-80 living alone without any care. What should we do to help them?"

Kaliq stood up from the chair to wash his hands "such people need our frequent visit. Do they have phone?" While washing his hand he said

"I doubt" Simon said

"Then we have to arrange one second hand instrument in the case of any emergency" Darshan said

"We will present this tomorrow after the yoga class and discuss. Now please permit me to leave" said good bye to all and left the place

A month later, Saleem visited the tribunal to appear before magistrate. All his children were present leant their heads in embarrassment. Upon identification the Magistrate began the hearing. The magistrate read out the history and verified evidence and the witness.

"Yes I remember the news on TV channel" The magistrate said and asked the son "do you have anything to say?"

"I admit my fault and accept the decision" Son said

"I sentence both husband and wife" then looked back in the application submitted by Kaliq on behalf of Saleem "Saleem, why do you want your son be acquitted from jail term?"

"He is my Son" Saleem said

"He and his wife bashed you brutally. I saw the marks in TV news. Oh... come on! Still you say he is your son." The magistrate asked

"But sir I am his father, how can I bear my own son being punished because of me" Simon said

"He and his wife are booked under IPC section 337, I cannot acquit them but on your written plea I may or may not, depends" the magistrate proceeded

Saleem saw the faces of his sons and daughter. All eyes were wet in pain gesturing despondent look asking forgiveness recurrently.

"I order all your children to pay rupees 8000 per month as maintenance allowance." The magistrate ordered all the children

The maintenance sum seemed too hefty but their guilt inhibited them to ask for consideration. However, Saleem's daughter moved her request, saying "Can you make a bit less so is not much hard"

The magistrate looked Saleem by gesturing eyes "what do you say?"

"Can she be freed from paying maintenance" Saleem asked

"What is this? Are you joking on Jury? Nonsense, don't want this don't want that, then why have you come for? You fool us?" The magistrate asked in annoyance

"No sir not that, the father's heart weeps seeing the tears in kid's eyes." Saleem dropped a few drops of tears from the eyes

"It is a court and not your bloody heart" the magistrate said before giving his final verdict "No criminal should escape. Let this be an example to the world that mistreating elders have a lesson to learn. Therefore, I order six months jail term to son and his wife, besides he shall pay one hundred thousand rupees to his victim father" and once again he looked Saleem and said "and rupees six thousand as maintenance allowance each month by each child. In case of failure to comply with you will be sentenced to jail term for 3 months." Magistrate before adjourning the procedure looked at Saleem and said "a soft man".

All the children felt respite from the embarrassing situation, hurting own father was more severe than the court ordered. The eldest son said *"we have exited safe from here but Allah will definitely punish us in our old age."*

The third son wept loudly and went straight to his father, knelt to touch his feet "I am a cruel animal. Please forgive me if you can."

"It is not I to punish or forgive. Allah decide will finalize" while saying Saleem raised him and kissed his head.

Shame to face father, tears in eyes pushed them back. Daughter showed bit courage, came close to Saleem and asked forgiveness. Another son in hesitation asked "I wish if you could live with us." But Saleem refused out rightly, said "no more please, so painful I can't take anymore, I trust none of you" before leaving them he introduced Azra "soon I will marry her" and joined his beloved friends and Azra.

Later in the evening Neelam as usual entered in the kitchen and asked husband "chop some potatoes and onion while I prepare gram flour solvent"

Preetam chopped onion in wet tears took wife's edge of sari to wipe off "onion is so hard makes all weep"

"But none uses sari to wipe" Neelam said, husband came closer and closer to arouse her by hugging and kissing.

"What are you doing? Papa will see" moved shrinking backward Neelam said in hesitance.

Preetam came out to check if father was around, found he was in the drawing room. Prem looked at son's eyes the erotic craving.

"I go for walk for five minutes and come back" Prem said

"Why dad? We are preparing Pakoda as snack with booze" though Preetam wished from inside the undisturbed freedom for quenching crave.

"Feel like" and Prem went outside to walk in his lush balcony.

It was enough for him to take advantage to unbutton her top and pull her sari up. Both took deep breath then cuddled each other, fell in deep emotional sensation. Each other's energy traveled through other's body to reach a state of mirth. It was the submission to caress the other. After all went well both kissed each other again.

Sexual craving drives a man or woman furiously mad until quenched. They have to quench without the interruption and meddling. Whoever is obstacle during the act is foe irrespective of any relationship. This irritation adds up into other small-small untoward incidences of botherations. Over time blows into spark to form into wild fire. Contrary to it, widow or widowers anywhere near to the sensual act, too get aroused, failing to quench drives to jealous and abhor. This is also one of the factors daughters in law and many a times son too hate aged parents.

Neelam after washing her hands placed bowl on the stove burner, poured mustard oil and waited to boil. In the meantime she added salt, chili powder, dry mango powder and parsley powder in gram flour solvent, stirred to mix well. Then dipped potatoes and onions into solvent and immersed into boiling oil. After preparing she came to drawing room with pakodas. Looked for Prem and sounded in loud voice "things are ready. Let's sit.

All assembled in drink session. Son opened a bottle, poured in two glasses and asked Neelam to share whisky with them.

"If you wish but I take very light with the juice" Neelam replied

Though Neelam was bit reluctant, said "remember never offer whisky too often to a woman as I said last time. She is prone to addiction easily, once she develops the taste, she cannot resist to alcoholism" after two three sips she felt so awful taste, she had to throw and fill with fresh juice into her glass "how do you bear this taste?"

Both Prem and Preetam laughed loudly and continued sipping the peg. After intake of two pegs Prem fell in deep thoughts and came with poem"

Company of rummer in solitude,
Refuge to my loneliness;
Flows the sorrow to tipsiness,
As lake water to the shore;
In exhilaration of libation,
Past cosy memories are alive;
Forget all hurt me once,
Forget all gave me pain;
As a ghostly night as past,
and dawn is alive;
Booze is company in my sad,
Makes me feel still I'm alive;
Rummer when kisses my lips,
A feel of love conjures my heart;
company of rummer in solitude,
Refuge to my loneliness;

Neelam was swift to ask "Did you love your wife?"

"Yes, but was beyond love. We never had ever said to each other 'I love you', yet her absence tortured us" while saying he fell in pain,

Neelam wasted no time to solace "your son and me both are always with you"

"I know, but, sometimes you miss something you can't exchange with children. You need someone deep of your age so you are very free. However, for me it's not a big problem as I am most of the time busy and in the evening busy with kids. Is this not a fortunate life for an aged man?" Prem said

"You are not aged yet" after pausing for a while Neelam again said "that reminds me, my mom said two days ago, she was feeling bored and asked me to visit her for a few days"

"No... No... you are not going anywhere" Preetam was worried while saying

"Why not? She is my mom!" Neelam retorted

"Why don't you call your mom here? She can stay here as long as she wants to stay. Am I right dad?" Preetam worried about her going to maternal house for so long. But, both did not realize the conspiracy to bond her mother and Prem together as Saleem.

"Yes, why not? It's our honor" Prem then took last piece of Pakoda from the plate.

Neelam could not trace the happiness in Prem's face. She thought in her mind "may be because memory of his past wife still overwhelms his mind. Similar

Live and let live

situation is with my mom too. At times she too feels grievous moments. They both want something I can give."

Prem took his last sip "today is too much. I took four pegs. Let us have dinner and I will go for sleep"

Sangeeta placed food on the table and served to Prem and sat beside Preetam. After finishing Prem washed his hand and went straight to bed. But Preetam and Neelam went to kitchen to clean plates and bowls. Then went to their bedroom to sleep in bed he caught her ear and said "I know how sharp you are? Do you think my father is fool?"

"I have a woman brain, think far beyond your thoughts reach" Neelam caught back his ear and said

"What if dad minds?" Preetam whispered

"Did he say 'No'?" Neelam said

"No" Preetam answered

"You men know nothing about domestic relationship, except the one best known to you is to spray sperm in women. And your job is over." Neelam said bantering Preetam.

She placed her right leg between Preetam's legs, laid right hand over shoulder and face over of chest of Preetam "How many times did you see him sitting alone in wet eyes?" Neelam asked

"Never"

"I have seen number of times, sometimes even drops in his eyes. Gestured me how sad he was" Neelam said

"Yes, we don't realize because we have. But when any of us miss we too dither in pain" Preetam accepted said again "I failed to witness my father's pain as am busy in office"

"With me he has limitations to mingle, but when you arrive in the house his cheek blossoms. I can't see your father gloom. Am I right?" Neelam said

"Yes" Preetam said in half sleep

"I am going to ask mama to join us this week. Get the room cleaned, ok!" Neelam asked again and again but he was asleep.

'A movie four whimsical friends'

The four friends sat back in the park, after some gossips made a program to watch movie in Chankya cinema. They all went to Prem's home where Neelam his daughter in law was busy cooking. Normally, she prepared breakfast for Prem separately after arriving from the Yoga class.

"Today we are four for the breakfast" Darshan said

Showing no fear she said "You see, I am not scared as long as you give a hand," she looked at his and Prem's face and smiled. Then she inquired from Prem whispering "what do I prepare?"

"Anything, easy to make" Prem replied

Neelam went inside and asked Prem to get some eggs from the shop next door. She poured water into the bowl to boil and added ten eggs into it. Came back and said "in ten minute egg curry and chapatti (bread) will be ready.

Prem went inside to assist her. While kneading flour by adding water Prem asked "do you wish to come to the movie with us?"

"Which movie"? Neelam asked

"'Four whimsical friends' in Chanakya hall"

"I know it is a super hit movie. Do you expect you get tickets?" Neelam said while adding spices into curry. Took a pinch of curry in the spoon and tasted and gave part to Prem "taste, is it ok?"

"It's good but you can add little bit more of salt" Prem said

"How can I come to watch movie with two kids" Neelam asked

"It's your wish, we are going for noon show" Prem said. However, Prem could observe her face of gesturing 'yes' from inside "I know you want"

He went to his gang "I think she too wishes though not yet opened up"

After the bread and the egg curry got ready. Darshan brought the plates and Saleem brought glasses of water. Simon prepared coffee and brought to the dining table. Prem took the food to the dining table.

Simon got his mobile phone out of pocket and called the Chanakya manager "we want five adult tickets and 2 infants for the noon show. Have those ready at hand and come to us in the main gate."

"Ok, but for infants under five years you don't need tickets. I wait for you" the manager replied

"Neelam, please get ready and get the children ready, I will wash dishes," then said while washing "We will have lunch outside." Prem said

"Hotel and food of your choice" Simon was swift to say

Live and let live

After finishing breakfast all came out for their homes to get ready except Saleem who went along with Darshan and said "look, she is also a daughter in law, behaves like she is daughter of Prem."

"No daughters or Mothers in laws are bad. The upbringing, environment, fear, ego, greed together contribute to conflicting situations. Many times Prem appreciated her for her behavior" Simon stated

"This reminds me their families were known to each other for a long time. This is likewise the reason the cordial relationship." Saleem said

"You can blame somewhat 'arrange marriage system', where the girl does not know him and his family. Parents only see the personality, background, financial potential, but no home atmosphere. In such situations you can know only after mingling for some time with their family. This is why traditional engagement prior to marriage is considered, but no one cares to allow boy and a girl going to experience each other and the family." Darshan while moving to his home presented his point of view.

"Yes you are truthful, including me, all the parents expect their daughters adjust in a new place. Fear of losing virginity of their daughters if allowed to play freely with engaged person scares them".

Darshan and Saleem got ready "what time is it?"

"Ten past half" Saleem said

"Ok let's go we have to pick all" Darshan came down to Pajero, opened the door and Saleem sat beside him, drove away to reach Prem's house. Reaching there they found Simon had not yet arrived. Darshan called Simon's mobile "Where are you Simon?"

"I may need some time, please reach there if I am bit late to collect the tickets from him. Don't pay any money I will tell him. Most likely I will reach timely" Simon said

"Ok, does he recognize me?" Prem asked

"Yes, we sat together in drink party"

"Yes, I recall today. Be sure to reach before time." Darshan said him

They did not have to wait for long for Simon. Prem held one kid in his lap and the other in the lap of Darshan. In appropriate time they went into the vestibule and sat in reserve seats.

After some advertisements the movie started, casted by Khan, Arora, Sharma and Richard. And in Actress side Priyanka, Saadia, Chitra and Merriam.

The introductory scene, Khan stands under a coconut tree having sip of cool drink. He does not know the coconut plucker sitting on top to extract wine, secretly watching his romantic flirt. Unexpectedly, a girl appears to be Arora's sister 'Priyanka'. He looked at her in inamorato gaze and began to comment raising his both hands above the shoulder "oh my sweety sweet...drop some nectar juice... But before finishing his saying a bunch of 6 coconuts falls on his

Live and let live

head injuring deep, he falls on the ground unconscious. His head and shoulder smash.

The second introductory scene of Richard a body builder isn't happy with one miss. He tried both Saadia and Priyanka but failed and now tries Sharma's sister 'Chitra'. Always wait and wait to have a glimpse of her. One day holding plantain in hand stands near the open manhole in his colony. Wait a glimpse of her; hurriedly eat a banana and throws off the peel in his front. He does not care the waste bin a few steps on his right. Once she appears while crossing the road, his mind works to bring out this song:

'O' my angel of paradise,
Is this thy lips,
Or is this rose;
Thy tears are sorbet,
Wish caress thee syrupy eyes;
Redolence of your sweat,
Strews ambiance,
Stimulates the feeling,
Of exotic love;
Your white bright complex,
Radiates the heaven,
Sprinkles lustrous ignis;
When you walk, its like,
Roe cool gait,
Fitted jean and top,
On your bust,
Waist and hip gestures,
Thou an ocean babe;
O' my angel of paradise,
Is this thy lips,
Or is this rose;

His lips are moving, eyes straight into her eyes, hands pointing in vacillating gait moves towards her crooning song. But don't realize he steps on the peel can hurl him down. He moves first step, then the second direct on the peel and glides straight into the manhole. Both legs and the arms are fractured and head suffers injury, rests in hospital.

The third introductory scene of the Arora Sikh boy wearing red turban, trouser, shirt and red Nike shoes, standing alongside of a wall in his erotic look. 'Saadia' Khan's sister looking beautiful appears crossing road to reach the bus stop. His eyes are straight into her sexy eyes, raising hands to flash a kiss. But the fighter bull tracks him in all red from far comes straight running to him, hits with his two horns and hurls ten feet high. A profusely bleeding rests in hospital bed.

The final introduction of scene of Sharma thinking 'wasted so many days, choosing which one he should go with'. He brought 'Priyanka' in his dream, but found interruption of Khan laying snag "she is sweet but looks she is stuff of

Khan" he wiped her from his mind. Then brought 'Chitra' in his dream, dreamed of her in the lush green park, together sat chatting, love was flying over the sky, he tried to lay his head in her lap was not so soft as he thought "No, she too I reject" he wiped her from his mind. He then brought 'Saadia' in mind, dreamed her in his dreams, she was great but found interruption during soothing love, Sikh Arora entering over and over with the Kirpan (knife) in the dream. He stood up from the bed in shock and said in mind "No war for a girl" wiped her too from his mind. He finally chose Richard's sister 'Merriam' as was untouched in everyone's dream.

He began to flirt, he looked at the watch at the appropriate time and said in mind "it's, time let me watch her exhilarating gait. Standing close to the building where she lives. She comes down to catch the bus. He whistles and sings a song to hold her notice:

I'm a flirt, love my aim,
Wander hither thither,
Like clouds full of rain,
Floats over vales and hills,
Till Empties load of drops;
I gleam brighten thee,
Like sun burns self,
To lighten world;
My aim is love,
Wander hither thither;
Like a lake flows,
Till the end of shore;
The passion of love,
Overwhelms my sole;
Over and over,
Pulsates my heart;
Sounds dhak, dhak,
Like current of ocean tide;
Flutter my hands,
As wings of birds;
Move legs, torso too move,
Dance like birds of paradise;
I'm a flirt, love my aim;

She turns back to look at him and with a smile she inclines her head and goes forward to bus stop. Sharma now jovial too follows her, all attention on her, no traffic, no left, no right but crossing road. A racing car smashes him, and he falls unconscious with multiple cracks.

81

Now the main movie starts. All are in different beds in same ward of hospital. There too they don't spare the nurse. Fed up of their flirting, annoyed nurse injects medicine with larger syringe on each, saying "this is for you flirts" then shows the size of syringe. "Oooh so big very painful, aaah..." all bounce off to catch the nurse but the painful move rest them back to the bed in one creepy voice "Oh God (in their religious tone) save us from women. They won't let us carry on"

After sometime when the situation calms, each lie half sleep in bed. Saadia comes to meet her brother with a fruit juice bottle in hand "hi! How are you" and sits beside him in the bed in direction to have a glimpse of poor Sikh Arora. He is looking pitiable both hands hung on supporting rods and head and all face covered with bandage except the eyes and lips. She gazes sympathetically at him though has no intention to patch up, his romanticism rises high and looks at her, finds love insight within himself.

Sikh Arora tries to rise but the pain snag pulls back to rest, crying "Oooh God what a pain."

Enviously Khan watches all episodes vigilantly. As is unable to move becks her to get closer and says "he is a con don't trust him. Moreover, we are Muslims have faith in Allah; our religion also says "who are not Islam are kafir."

"Are you sure?"

"Yes, you can check in Quran" Khan Replies

"Are you not giving me your misconcepted version of holy Quran?"

"No...no never" Khan Replies

Saadia retorts "then why do you flirt on his sister?" stands up in anger.

Khan closes eyes in blush with no reply. Somehow he manages to gains nerve, says "it's she who is after me, not me! I don't care non Muslims" says in scorny tone and watches her eyes expecting her understanding.

"Shut up, you idiot liar" and slaps on his face before leaving in anger.

Next moment Priyanka enters the ward with some grape in her hand. She discusses with the nurse the well being of her brother. Looks they are friends for long time, then goes straight to her brother.

"Hi, how are you?" sits beside her brother Arora in the direction so can watch poor Khan whispering ooooh...ooooh in pain. For some time he did not notice as was in severe pain, but, sweet tone of her, unexpectedly relieves all pain in him. Gazes at her adoringly and gestures his gratitude for her visit by moving eyes and face. She gives a look at Khan sympathetically and smiles.

"Thanks Allah, you are great" Khan whispers and shrugs his arms in pain "Ooh, Allah is this time for you to give me pain. Please be quite for some time"

Priyanka turns her face to her brother who was watching enviously cozy gap between two. She places some grapes on the plate and slowly-slowly tries to feed. "No more grapes, I want Kirpan (knife). Please bring tomorrow."

"Why?" Priyanka asks

"I want to kill you both. I hate Muslims; he will convert you to wear a veil. You know Muslims are different humans, there is no match, and still you are flirting around him" Arora says in anger

"You dirty ass, then why do you flirt on his sister" Priyanka makes up her mind to teach him a lesson.

She goes straight to her nurse friend and asks her dress for a few minutes. She changes dress concealing her identity by hiding her face with virus protection cover, comes to Khan. She first comes to Khan and gives a smile. Khan goes mad and takes her to rasp his hand for pain alleviation. She knocks the rod support and stifles strongly the pain area till he shouts "Ooooh… Oooh…Ooh… oh you shit, give pain."

And so she gets straight to Sikh brother. But the ruttist brother tries to embellish her soft lovely hand. Stunned Priyanka shoves backward and uncovers her face "is this in your mind, you shameless?" And lashes a slap on his face before leaving.

Blushed Arora shuts his eyes, but Khan in pain joyously "ha… ha… ha" laughs teasing him.

The movie now shows flash back their past in flashback. In fact, they are very close friends since the childhood. Work in same place, but cabal to each other. Never waste a single chance to frame plot for each other in the workplace or anywhere they were together.

Once the boss ordered Khan to complete the file same day. Bushed Khan never expected the hard job. Richard to take the situation to his advantage hid some important information. Later when Khan failed to submit, boss scolded and asked Richard to complete the file. Both stared each other but Arora in anger and Richard in teasing smile.

One day while paying cricket the competition intensified among four friends. Richard lost patience on Sharma's continues sixes, kept all rules of bowling at stake he threw ball with force on the face of Sharma. Sharma was injured.

In the past too once Khan in his bike, shared a seat with Richard and Arora on his bike, shared a seat with Sharma drove at uncontrolled speed competing each other. Suddenly they saw two sweet girls in a car; one was driving and the other one chatting. The group of four lost the patience and gave a chase. The instinct in them ascended to show they were better than girls invited unwanted fate. The speeding bike overtook the car, but did not realize the transport bus was going ahead of them. Both the motorcycles rammed into the moving bus and sustained severe injuries.

Now we are in the present time in the movie… They are in the bed for the past eight months and ready to move out of the hospital. All are on stretchers, gloating each other walk away of the infirmary.

However animosity they possess, yet never forget to meet each other in a park close to house confirms the affection they have. In most of their talk, the major topic is a girl and portraiture of beautiful girls. Hence this time too they are discussing the same, then end up in arguments and skirmish.

One day, they gathered in the park, one of them saw an aged roughly seventy years old sorting from waste bin, beside him was his dog. Gang of four together goes limping to check. In shock Sharma asks "what are you doing?"

"Looking for food" the aged says

All in ruth pull out their purses from back pockets and try handing over money to him "take this?"

"For how many days, one, two or ten, then what?" Aged begins his search again, a bit of a pause and says again "then same back days to waste bin"

"Do you come each day?" Arora asks

"Yes" the aged replies

"Don't you have children to support?" Arora asks

"Never married, When I was young never realized this period also comes in the life. Nevertheless, I have so many unwanted children in the streets. I get money from scrap and spend on them."

"A very good idea" Richard said in appreciation

"I don't need an appreciation, what I want, is, those children don't suffer as I suffer. I also advise you my children this is a lesson for you too. *Never waste your young age to repent future.*"

"You should have married in appropriate period" Arora asks

"Mother died after delivering me and father when I was six."

Now the movie flashes back to his past background... Aged waste picker reached the 10th year of his life, worked in small eatery house endured hard job, worked right from morning at four till night 12. Even then he was happy as food, shelter, clothing and security with affection from the proprietor. He worked until the owner passed away. Before dyeing the owner handed over the shop to him and said "now it is your time to run the show". He managed for 6 years until the shop was demolished by the local authority for the elaboration of the road. As he did not hold any professional aptitude, he had to move with his traditional street tea shop. He carried the show for some time and fed the family of the ex - owner and himself. There too he had to bear the jerk of fate, the administration dismantled his stall.

The movie continues to show present state. The aged man in bit of tears scrubbing eyes with dirty hands "You know, some people are like that, born ill-fated and dye like that. There was no one to guide me to think beyond. I was busy in eatery house in young age had never thought of moving beyond. I was so careless with my life. In spare time watched movies. Though I was happy with my limited desires, yet never realized the world moves and moves to reshape self." Then inclines to sort the waste to find food for his dog.

Gesturing towards the sitting dog next to him, the aged says "I picked up this dog from the street. Since then he is with me. He is my friend and kin too. All my good or bad times I share with him" then he bends down to look in the waste. After a while he again says "I have one more lifeless friend. I play flute and drum when I am alone with my dog" he pulls out to play.

"You play very well. Why don't you teach children" Richard says

"I have never thought of this" The aged says

"This is your education you can teach kids" Richard says

"Why did you not accept money we offered? You can use them for your street kids" Sharma asks

"I want to use my own hard earned money" Aged says

"Will you come tomorrow" Arora asks

"Yes, your locality is rich, waste lot of food, fruit and bread. I get lunch and dinner some times for me and my dog"

This day is the turning point of transformation for all four scoundrels. Spirituality and compassion together overwhelm all.

"We have to save him, it's our future too" Khan says and all others consent his master plan.

They then go to the police station to ask the cooperation. They enter the station limping. The police Inspector shouts in laugh "oh…oh finally the gang of flirts here. What have you done this time?"

"We have come to seek your help" Khan asks humbly

"No way," the inspector stood up from the chair to reach them, holding Khan's ear tight asks "Tell me what you have done?"

"We accept, in the past we were wrong, but now we are here for other purpose" Khan precariously says

"What?" The inspector asks swiftly moving backward to sit back in his chair

"We want to help for an aged" Khan says

"How" inspector retorts

"He is a great musician plays flute and drum." Khan affirms

The inspector remains silent, thinking "Emm" thinks for a while again "I appreciate your effort towards ameliorating. Let me see what I can do" A pause, then says "come tomorrow with him"

The next day they first come to the aged and explain their proposal. The aged accepts saying "in this old age if I am still worth it is my privilege" and accompanies to the police station.

The police inspector inquires his background to make sure he is not a criminal and spares a space to conduct to teach the street kids. The first music class begins with his flute song,

I fly over vales and hills,
Like a moisten cloud,
Hover over ocean,
Hover over lush bush;
Embellishes feather,
kisses my beak,
'O' my lovely dove,
Take my love,
Give this kiss,
To my lovely prince,
The kiss she gives,
Embellishes my fur,
Are not for me;
I carry her love and kiss,
Like the clouds carry drops,
Wander hither, thither,
Pours its shower,
Over lake and barren land;
Prince too waits return of me,
As thirsty barren land;
He too holds me,
Gives kiss on my cheek,
Like a messenger,
I take his kiss,
pour in princess lips;
I am messenger,
Seek a kiss and pass it on;

The gang of four too sit there holding flute in hand, wink on each other, but each other's sisters in their flashback dream and speak out "*The waste too has something to teach, provided you have will to learn*" The movie ends

"First I thought the movie is rubbish" Simon said

"The last has something" Neelam adds to Simon's

Live and let live

Both Prem and Neelam reached home. Neelam's mother was already, sitting outside, asked "I have been waiting for over two hours. Where were you?"

"We went to watch movie" Prem said, looked for the keys and opened the door. Neelam took baggage and placed in 3rd room.

Her mom got fresh and went straight inside the kitchen to cook for the evening. Neelam watching all said to Prem "the laws are starting to shift today. We will have good food, dresses washed, house cleaned. But controlled by her."

"Yes I see this" Prem said

"For long you were never under control" Neelam said in teasing tone

"She is a woman and wants her control" Prem said then laughed loudly

Neelam too laughed "oh... Yeeee..."

Neelam's mother 'Komal' came out of kitchen said "we don't have potatoes, no onion and no chilly left. How you had managed like this?"

In fact, Komal's freedom in this house was more than in her son's house. She was taking full advantage to adorn the home.

"We managed well" Prem and Neelam said together

"Ok, now go and buy something" 'Komal' the mom thought for a while and said "you people know nothing. I will also come"

 "I can't, I am exhausted. You go alone" Neelam said

"I am new to this place, how can I" Komal reverted

"If papa agrees you can take him with you." Neelam said. But Komal bashfully ran to the kitchen and Prem gazed at Neelam disgracefully. Eventually they both agreed to visit vegetable market.

That day something had happened, heat wave was cool, stars twinkled in day light. Initially a bit of shy then opened up as the full moon at night. Came closer and closer, walked side by side. It was one hour, two and then three hours to buy vegetable.

This was the moment Neelam waited, said to Preetam "how many hours have lapsed since you arrived from the office?"

"Almost two hours. What?" Preetam asked

"Nothing" Neelam whispered

When both arrived, were looking happy, smiles in both the faces. Eyes were flashing like sun shine of dawn. Komal went straight to kitchen helped by Prem.

Live and let live

Neelam pinched Komal's arm and said "so you first sow, then waited to grow till the vegetable bloomed, then plucked and brought to farm. Am I right?"

"Shut up" Komal just gloated

"Do you like him?" Neelam asked

Komal nodded "yes, since long time, even before my marriage"

"Then why did you not marry him?" Neelam asked

"It is a long story. Don't remind me" Komal said

"Did you meet him before?" Neelam asked

"Yes, we met and talked together several times in family parties"

"Why did this not heave?" Neelam asked

"May be he did not understand hidden love inside me or I failed to reveal. Something happened, I don't know" Komal said

"Did you ever repent?" Neelam asked

"After I got married I found your father a better man and I forgot the past" Komal replied

"Why did you not tell this to me before?" Neelam asked

"Are you idiot? How can I tell my own daughter that I loved someone" Komal said

"But we were like friends" Neelam said while kissing her cheek

"There has to be some distance between daughter and the mother" Komal said

Preetam too came to scene, said to Neelam "your strategy worked very well"

Neelam simply smiled and asked Preetam to get ready for celebration. Neelam and Komal together got snacks ready. Preetam came to Prem's room with bottle of whisky.

Prem was busy playing with children said "not today. What will she think?"

Preetam came straightway to Neelam "Papa said not today"

"Why" Neelam asked

"Because of your mom"

"Nothing doing" Neelam came straight to Prem, said in childish style "Today is our celebration day. We will…"

"For me no problem, but think of your mother. Will she not be upset?" Prem said

Then she went to Preetam "When you pour juice add some alcohol in mom's glass. Don't forget"

The drink session started. First sip gave different taste to Komal "What is this taste? Do you think I will not know?" She gazed at Preetam and continued "anyway I like it"

"Little bit of whisky mixed in the juice" Preetam agreed

However, Komal enjoyed drink and asked for another peg, said "after fifty years of age without a companion to share one resorts to taking little bit to relax. Although I admit in long term is hazardous. However, sometimes this is recourse to my loneliness"

Later on two pegs, drunken Komal revealed her past history "You know, before my marriage, I had loved someone without giving any clue to that man"

Prem pointed his figure towards Neelam, asked "she is drunk at once"

But Neelam gestured by winking eyes and moving lips "please let her say" and came closer to Prem "let her unravel concealed love"

"Ok" Prem then directed Preetam to pour more. Preetam made one more peg for him.

Komal too asked for one more peg but this time Neelam winked at Preetam and poured pure juice in the glass

"Why the taste changed?" Komal asked after sipping

"It's because you are drunk" Prem said

Komal laughed at Prem "Are you joking? Do you remember, once you with your friend visited the party hosted by my father? How many pegs did I take that day, do you have any idea?"

She took a sip and said again gazing Prem "I am so lonely after your friend died."

Then she gave a look at Neelam "Prem's that friend was your father. I miss him"

In whole episode Prem kept silence. But Neelam wanted him to speak out, that she managed "do you remember anything of mom's past?"

"She was naughty and cheerful. I liked her but not in that depth. Perhaps because your mother in law occupied that space before" Prem said

"Many a times I saw your wet eyes, sitting alone in balcony. Was it because you could not share your pain with us?" Neelam asked

Prem kept silence but her persuasion coerced him to say "I remember Pooja (wife) off and on, after her death loneliness dispirited me"

"Same situation I endure so many times" Komal said

"Now I think though can't replace your partners, yet you will have something in common to share old occasions" Neelam said to Komal

Common sharing incidences between old friends evolved to love and then the odor of flourishing garden. The nest was once again a home for all. Both Komal and Prem controlled the home. It wasn't home but paradise of Prem and Komal, and Preetam and Neelam.

The following day was thick cloudy dawn; strewed flash of thunder, the sound was like bursting squib, maybe a sign of mirth on recovering Saleem. Entire ambiance was florid; the birds were tweeting song:

'O' my sweetheart,
'O' my sweetheart...
Your love is deep,
As dense cloudy dawn;
intense depth of love,
As black hole in sky;
Has so much gravity,
Drags me into
Your marshy mash;
Once I'm in, can't pull out;
As light from black hole
can't get out;
'O' my sweet heart...
Your beauty is
thundering light,
Strews all over,
my body and heart;
'O' my sweetheart...
Your caress charges,
as lights from thundering clouds;
your deepest love,
Sounds like thundery flash,
Perhaps a sign of mirth,
gives me soothing touch;
'O' my sweetheart...
Your love is bond,
Like tiny droplets,
Of opaque clouds;
Coerce me, cohere you always;
'O' my sweetheart...
You give me hope,
As wet loam of earth,
by drizzling drops from clouds;

Live and let live

Shankar held his palms together and wished "Namaskaar! Today, as the ground is wet, we are going to perform standing exercise. The figure of this yoga is 'Konasna'." He stood up straight and directed to perform "Stand straight with feet approximately hip width distance apart and arms alongside the torso. Breathe in and raise the left arm up so that the fingers point towards the roof. Breathe out and turn to the right, first from the spine, and then move your pelvis to the left and bend a little more. Hold your left arm pointing upwards. Bend your head to look upwards at the left palm. Straighten the elbows. Breathing in, straighten your body back up. Breathing out, bring the left arm down. Repeat the same with your right arm"

In the midst of exercise rain began pouring to hinder Yoga exercise "I think today is not a day to continue our yoga practice" Shankar said as others were running to find cover.

Mostly all left except the key members, assembled at Darshan's house to discuss the past updates of visits to aged people. A three storied building with 12 rooms and the roof had 2 more rooms. A division of the mansion he had let out to renters. Drawing room had enough space to accommodate all, one by one sat on the beautiful sofas. A little later servant brought coffee.

"Prepare some breakfast for all of us" Darshan asked while accepting coffee.

"What do you prefer to eat?" The servant asked while counting the number of people

"Whatever, you can make fast?" Darshan asked

"Ok, will make potato and onion stuffed parattas and basil, mint, onion chutney" the servant moved fast by saying and yelled at coworker "go, bring some curd and butter from the dairy"

The woman cook prepared floor by adding a little salt, asked senior one "please tat this while I boil potatoes."

The cooking process was at full speed. Here in drawing room all looked busy gossiping. Simon took a newspaper lying on the stool and unwrapped to read. Read the first page, second page, but on the third page he became more attentive read out loudly "aged husband and wife were murdered, the motive behind was burglary."

"Off and on such incidences are happening. Ridiculous, what the police and its beat officers do?" Prem said

"Police are slack" Simon answered

Azra took 'the Times of India' newspaper cutting from her handbag and read out "National Crime Records Bureau (NCRB) shows that more than 1,100 senior citizens were murdered while just as many were robbed. The act of such crimes came second only to cheating, which claimed over 1,500 elderly victims. NCRB has for the first time tabulated data on crimes against senior citizens. According to the data for 2014, the number of elderly were killed in UP (174), Tamil Nadu (173) and Maharashtra (170). Among large states, Bihar and Odisha turned out to be safest for senior citizens with elderly murder rates per one lakh of population in these states being recorded at 0.2 each. As many as 58 rapes were committed on elderly women across the country last year. Of these nine were committed in Maharashtra, six in Kerala and five each in Madhya Pradesh and Rajasthan."

"The sharp rise in burglary and murder of the elderly population is a serious concern. The appropriate Governments need to consider and bring forward the solution" Darshan remarked

"Scary figure of Delhi" Darshan said

Paramjeet a former employee of NGO gave another figure from world ageing population "Over 100 million over the age 60 of today is likely to grow nearly 400 million by 2050. Of this, 45% have chronic disease and 50% of diabetic in India are elderly. Over half a million elderly die of tuberculosis every year. Over 60% of elderly population lives in poverty and 80% lack medical and health care. All as a result of lack of medical and pension to informal sector workers. After hard work of all life they end up in old age poverty. Should they not be entitled to Social security benefits as in formal sectors?"

"Many efforts have been done and laws have been passed yet there is a room for improvement. Nearly 70% of the elders don't know the availability of the vantage. Nearly 60% don't even know they are protected under Senior Citizens Act 2007. Introduction of Law isn't itself complete unless each elderly is informed the rights and procedures." A medical Practitioner 'Arjun' newly joined, said

"I have seen elderly of 80 standing in queue in hospitals, ration distribution centers and banks for pension. It is injustice as are weak, unable to walk or stand in a waiting line. The Act needs to bring guidelines to seek help of Palliative care mobile units and mobile banking system to ease their problems." Darshan said.

"Chapter 3 & 4 of the Act clearly mentions the set up of old age homes. But failure to follow up has resulted disappointment. Each Government, NGO and Private run hospital having over 25 beds need to have old age homes. They may charge from who can ante up the luxury. Ratio 1: 2: 3 Luxuries: medium (minimal charge): and poor (free): For childless elderly old age home is very helpful as they have no-one to help" A medical Practitioner 'Arjun', said

Arjun waited for a while and again brought up "for childless or support less elders we can seek aid of close by school or college students to liaise with them in order to create affinity ambiance."

"This is a sound idea, CBSE and UGC can introduce as an assignment with marks essential for prospects in board examinations. The process may need longer, we will wait not until then and visit the schools for their participation in our mission" Iyyer said

"Penalty and punishment under this act need to be raised further as 3 months and Rs. 5000 is very low amount, easily affordable to escape from the liability. The objective of the law should be to coerce children take responsibility, nothing compared to the amount and the time the aged had spent throughout their life span raising them." Aabidah said

"Senior Citizen Act 2007 says a lot, but the follow up nil. I have never seen the block police or corporation units visiting any senior citizen's home." A medical Practitioner, said.

Prem continued "anathema of seniors is serious. In half a dozen out of 10 houses we visited had one mode or the other suffer mental torture and disparagement, is unknown and concealed cruel domestic violence"

Kaliq said, showing the registration letter to all "Now we are registered society, need an office and full time working people. The most important is the fund."

"As far as office is, you can use my residence. However, I feel Darshan's house is centrally situated and easy reachable." The Judge stated

Darshan went inside saying "I'm honored", picked a bundle of 100's currency notes. "Let us start from me, rupees ten thousand towards my contribution. In the front room, I will lay some chairs and tables with telephone connection."

"We together and beneficiaries will definitely contribute a contribution. After giving result, we can approach the Government for grant" Kaliq said

Pointing ladies Kaliq said "Minimum one man who can devote full time service. We will print notices indicating mobile numbers of all active members. Our presence of easy accessibility to domestic crisis will reveal our reliability and strength."

The judge thought for sometime then said "I will not be available for full time, same with Kaliq and some office goers."

Two women raised their hands to show their willingness to offer full time participation. "We sit without work at home, can come and join the service" Aabidah and Paramjeet both said

"I have worked with an NGO in the past. It's my honor to make use from past experience" Paramjeet said

Breakfast odor all over the sitting room gestured was time for the feast. "Oh! Very nice smell of pure cow butter and hot mango pickle" Judge took a piece from paratta with curd and in a spoon Mint-basil chatnee "Superb and very spicy, we south Indians love spicy food"

Simon while chewing the piece updated from the past story narrated in the hospital "The poor aged couple live in one room and rest of the rooms have let out to tenants. Now the tenants are neither paying dues nor are they vacating the house"

"Why did they not go to the police?" Aabidah asked

"We did not discuss everything. Can go again with the Judge and the Kaliq for detailed information" Simon said

The breakfast was over; all got their hands washed, sat back on the sofa for detailed discussions.

Darshan said "we need to help the childless couple"

"Old Age helplessness"

The Judge stood up and asked the team to follow to their house. They knocked the door and waited for some time to open. Gloomy face Aged couple at the door, very scared of witnessing a group of people asked "what do you want?"

"Do you remember? We came last time" Darshan said

"Yes… Yes" aged man recollecting memory

"Can we enter? " Prem asked

"Sure" aged lady said

One by one all hugged and held their hands to soothe. Chitra supported them to the cot "please sit"

"But you…" the aged man said

"Don't worry, we are ok" Chitra humbly requested

Emotional tears in their eyes "thanks for the kindness"

Priya took her hankie and wiped the dropping tears "please smile now"

The aged childless couple said "surviving with the meager pension"

"You don't have relatives" Priya asked

"Yes, we have the relatives; they want our property but not us. We are unlucky people. No one even comes to visit us" the aged man said.

Priya sat beside them, her arm over shoulder of aged lady tried soothing to lower soreness.

Kaliq called tenants to join the conversation and asked the couple "how long they have been staying with you?"

Aged lady replied "Nearly ten years" that tenant consented by saying "Yes"

"Do you give, rent receipt?" Kaliq asked

"No" the aged lady said

"How long you have not been paying rent" Kaliq asked the tenant

"Nearly for six months" tenant replied crouching head, and then gazed at aged expecting their accord.

"No… He is lying. It's over two years. When we ask, he is always ready with violence, misbehavior and shouts at us" the lady said

"We doubt, they possess forged documents of my property" the aged man said

"Do you know? You can be booked under the senior citizen Act, protection of life and Property of senior citizen and separately Indian Penal Code Section 327- 329. You will have no way out to escape" Kaliq warned him

With ridicule smile staring Kaliq the tenant said "Don't threat me please; I am very much aware of our court procedures and judgment delays. The corruption in the court helps make the verdict longer as long as we want. My question is will these idiots survive till the judgment?"

The tone was challenging the team. An insult to the judiciary none could expect, decided them to show the reliability of the judiciary.

"Well, my boy, so, you have already planned a plot to grab this house. Do you think you can do easily?" Darshan

Kaliq looked at the judge and said "looks he isn't easy man, this master of crimes need a lesson"

Tenant's wife joined him and said "we have been living in the house for the past ten years. It is not easy to evict us."

"Does this guarantee you the ownership?" Kaliq replied

The judge asked to pass his phone and called police commissioner "I am High Court Judge Iyyer here. I want your help"

Answered from the other side "what do you want me to do?"

Judge said "call the deputy commissioner with his team to reach, the address I SMS you"

"Ok" the other side replied

"Sorry sir, we never knew your position. Please forgive us, will vacate the house as soon as possible" the tenant said and his wife knelt to touch judge's feet

In frightened face and trembling legs, held their palms together pleaded "please don't punish us. My husband has been unemployed for 3 years, that's the reason we did not pay her rent. Trust us; we are no criminals, our helplessness with no other option coaxed to act like this"

"But it doesn't look like. You live a posh life. Neck full of gold necklaces, hand full of gold bangles and 3 of five fingers of each hand, in your ear diamond studded ring. You say your husband is unemployed." Chitra asked

An alarm of the police jeep cautioned all neighbors. Deputy Commissioner got down, straightway entered and shook hand with Kaliq his old friend. Kaliq introduced him with the judge Iyyer.

They together discussed the situation in depth and asked the circle inspector "please prepare first investigation report" inspector took noting from aged couple and showed to the deputy commissioner. Kaliq too had a glance and asked "add defaming judiciary in front of 15 persons, including the high court judge and the advocate"

Both tenant and his wife pleaded over and over "forgive us. Don't punish us please, we will be nowhere." Finally, both knelt down, touching feet of Judge.

"It is too late now. Top of all, you have humiliated the Judge and all of us" Kaliq said

Judge took Kaliq to the corner and said quietly, "I smell something wrong with the tenant. Looks to me woman isn't normal" Kaliq gave gesturing look to the deputy commissioner.

Deputy Commissioner came close to the inspector and said quietly, "The doubts about their lavish life without earning for several years actuate to investigate. Can you please ensure the reality?"

"I have already investigated, sir, this house is the best point of her flesh trade" Inspector said

Kaliq silently said "this case isn't easy going. The tenant is clever, knows such cases call for time. Then our effort shall be to influence them to vacate house within the workweek. And focus on establishing criminal charges for assaulting aged and insulting judiciary."

Inspector framed the charges against both husband and wife, asked them to accompany him to the police station. There, the conversation got heated annoying him to ask the constable to put them behind the cell. Neither chair nor toilet inside had to beg for using to relieve was humiliating. Had to lie down along the floor, mosquitoes and bug stings added to already in trouble. They never had seen such a state of affairs.

Losing patience, the tenant asked the inspector "can I make a call to advocate friend of mine?"

"No" Inspector said

"Why not?" The tenant asked

"Because this isn't a property of your father, you son of a bitch" Inspector furiously shouted at him

"You will regret" the tenant retorted

"What for? You pimp of your wife" Inspector said

She shouted in anger immodestly "You son of a bitch, how can you speak like this. I can take your ass through women court"

In India, prostitution (the exchange of sexual services for money) is not illegal, but a number of related activities, including luring in a public place, owning or managing a brothel, prostitution in a hotel, pimping and pandering, are crimes. Prostitution is legal only if carried out in the private dwelling of a prostitute. However, under 'section 7 (sub section 3) ITPA Act 1956 the appropriate Government may direct that the prostitution shall not be carried on in such area or areas as may be specified in the notification'. Which are within a distance of two hundred meters of any place of public religious worship, educational institution, hotel, hospital, nursing home or such other public place of any kind as may be notified in this behalf by the Commissioner of Police or Magistrate in the manner prescribed, shall be punishable with imprisonment for a term which may extend to three months.

The inspector had already investigated about them before reaching the spot. Collected evidences of running brothel behind door were clear enough for charges under an immoral traffic Act in public places within 150 meters of school and 200 meters of the temple. Inspector arranged her clients to reach police station, including the advocacy coordinator of the flesh trade. All six clients were present in another room. First, he called the advocate.

"How many times you laid her under you?" Staring at both husband and wife Inspector asked the advocate.

Advocate was already familiar with the inspector's barbarity. The inspector was very famous for his fierceness. This inspector was transferred several times for cruel conducts and many a time he disobeyed his superiors.

The advocate thought in the mind "nothing can stop from his brutal beating. If he finds foul conspiracy I too will become his victim."

"Some two, three times, but she is my money tree" advocate said

The inspector called all one by one. Took their statements in writing, forcefully occupying a house of senior citizens for use of the brothel, they are the clients visit periodically for sexual craving, and asked "be present when called"

All departed, but he called the advocate back "You are an advocate and very well aware of Section 18 under ITPA. I expect your cooperation for persuading them to vacate the house without any plot." The advocates turned back to move, but the Inspector called him back and yelled "and also tell them to pay their dues"

"I have given you everything in writing; itself is a witness enough to punish offenders?" The advocate said

"I warn you, the big shots are involved in this case" Inspector said

"Ok, I knew as a coordinator I am in trouble" the advocate said

"You have to stay back here till I say to go" Inspector ordered the advocate than he stood from his chair, went straight to the cell staring at the lady and the tenant "you bitch" and yelled in droll "Oh yeah!"

Then inspector asked the police constable "she expects nice behavior from us"

The lady police went inside the cell and gave no time to think, she began bashing her till she fainted. Then she came to the man and displayed her judo technique till he sat in pain.

Bashing continued till evening. Finally, they surrendered "we will do whatever you want"

"What you endured today is nothing before the pain you gave to poor aged, had been enduring for the past few years. Clear evidence to prosecute you under immoral Act and the senior citizen Act" The inspector said

"Now tell me what is the way out" tenant asked from the cell

"I don't think there is any way out as today is Saturday. You will have to remain here, even tomorrow." The inspector said

"How should I proceed getting rid of jail term" The tenant asked

You have to pay for humiliating the top brasses. There isn't any way out." The inspector said

Each two hours the lady constable entered and scolded in strong expletive words. For tenants wasn't easy relief, even begging wasn't accepted.

The lady constable said "here, nobody is going to see or hear anything. We are only doing the best to prepare you to endure the pain in jail. Prisoners hate the whores and the torturers of seniors." blew a slap on her face and said again "you did a worst blunder."

For them the hope from advocate too had waned. Conversing together the painful experience, blaming God the tenant said "we shouldn't have harassed the old shits"

"I will have no choice but to commit suicide when released after all the humiliation" cursing him she said

"You always blamed me since the day of my unemployment" the tenant said in lamenting voice

"Shame on you, are you a husband? Offering own wife to strangers for money." The tenant's wife was furious while saying, wiped her eyes with edge of the sari. She waited for a moment to recover from sobbing then she spat on her husband's face, said in a hissing voice "I piss on you, son of a bitch"

The inspector observed their reaction for the whole day. Constable handed two cups of tea and said "day after tomorrow we will present you before the judge. Your charges are serious, pray your God for any relief"

They both were exhausted the painful exercise and surrendered "please tell us what we need to do?"

She said "You may have to offer heavy sum"

"How much" the tenant asked

"Let me check with the inspector" she said and went to the Inspector to check

"Do you want me to tell you the amount? Four hundred thousand rupees" Inspector said

"It is too much" the tenant said

"Then I can't help as I have to share with from top to bottom" The inspector said. Both tenant and wife did not realize the conspiracy of the Inspector.

The lady constable went inside the cell and began bashing until they fainted "she said they are very tough"

"Can you please settle for 1.5 hundred thousand rupees" the tenant asked

"No..." the inspector said

"We have to be tougher to get the final. Such idiots assume we are fools and always after money. We too have mother and father." The inspector called the lady constable said

"Their actions have already revealed they belong to hell" the lady constable said

A ring in phone lady constable picked the phone and attended and handed over to Inspector "It's a call from Deputy Commissioner"

Inspector reached swiftly and picked "yes sir, we are progressing, we can even arrange compensation to the aged"

"Ok, you release them on Monday on condition they move out of house same day. Make them pay the dues to the elders" the Deputy Commissioner said

The inspector called the advocate coordinator "go and tell them the consequences"

The advocate went straight to them and said "if you don't vacate the house and pay due back to the aged, there is no way out."

"I am here in the lock up. How can I?" The tenant said

"Please do what I say. If you want I can go and shift your households to another place" the advocate said

"As you wish" the tenant said

"And how about their dues, how many months?" Advocate asked

The tenant memorized and said "rupees 8000 per month for 2 years and eight months"

"Two hundred and fifty six thousand" the advocate gave the figure

"You pay from your side and will pay back when out from here" the tenant agreed

The advocate coordinator approached the inspector "he agreed, will vacate the house tomorrow and give the due sum."

"Give result" Inspector thought for a while "now you can go."

The Inspector after confirming the house was emptied and the due amount was paid to the elders. On Sunday the tenants were released on condition in writing that they would never ever hold out or visit even near to elder's house. Then he personally visited the elderly couple to show support. Besides, he called Palliative care for timely health care.

The ambiance of next dawn was cool, as was content. Sun strewed its warmth gleam to this part of world. The birds too were happy tweeting lovely song:

Twee…Twee,
Twi…twiti…twi;
We are birdie sing a song,
Wake up Sun,
It's time to work;
Ghostly night gone,
Was past,
Now in bright side of life;
'O' my Sun give us warmth,
Glisten us with your ignis;
Twee…Twee,
Twi…twiti…twi;
Florets they bloom,
Wet in ravishing dew,
Strewing tipsy scent;
Wavy breeze cooling us,
We flutter dance;
It's a time beak to beak,
We are birdie sing a song,
Twee…Twee,
Twi…twiti…Twi;

All were present Saleem and Azra too. Today they were the talk of the town. All had eye on both of them. Shankar came with his CD player "today our exercise is inebriation on music. The music has so much of the power to draw the mind towards enchantment, joggles to immerse in the heavenly world, fumbling moments of blissfulness raises the desire to live."

He before switching on the player in full volume "Now we all close our eyes for a minute then concentrate on the music only. Then open eyes to view surrounding." All were dancing around in fun enjoying the blissful moment. Each one looking at each other's smiling face, all were in spiritual tipsy. After half an hour of dance Shankar gestured to halt "this exercise for relaxation relieves the stress, thus we stop when you feel tired."

Shankar was looking a bit exhausted owing to a convention till late night. "I think we end hear for today and come to another subject on social issues"

A social study student of master's degree came forth to explain his study on aging people, said "The aged have more to say and exchange past experiences with a new generation, but no one around tortures them. Loneliness is the grievous concern of aging people. Their lifespan is like in a dark room of the jail; endure painful isolation in the absence of own kin. Many blame modern time struggle to survive spurred children migrate overseas in search of jobs. Many say even when they are at home unable to dispense with time. I recently conducted survey in old age homes and cities and found worrying facts: Over 60% in semi & urban cities aged agreed they were conned by their own kids. Over 60 percent aged living with children believe they were alone in spite of living with them. 70% aged parents of migrant children agreed they were alone as their children were abroad or out of the urban center. Over 70 year age is the most affected, but women are ahead in victimization. However, ageds living with own spouses are content and happy. Those who have friends of the same age are as happier as living as a couple. Loneliness is like an epidemic disease rising day by day, taking toll of mental peace of many seniors. Living alone without anyone drives fear and mental stress influences the mental health"

Paramjeet took a printed paper of 'WHO mental health and older adults' from her hand bag and read out the grievous facts "The world's population is ageing fast. Between 2015 and 2050, the proportion of the world's older adults is estimated to almost double from approximately 12% to 22%. In absolute terms, this is an expected increase from 900 million to 2 billion people over the age of 60. Older people face special physical and mental health challenges which need to be acknowledged.

Over 20% of adults aged 60 and over suffer from a mental or neurological disorder (excluding headache disorders) and 6.6% of all disability (disability adjusted life years-DALYs) among over 60s is attributed to neurological and mental disorders. These disorders in the elderly population account for 17.4% of Years Lived with Disability (YLDs). The most common neuropsychiatric disorders in this age group are dementia and depression. Anxiety disorders affect 3.8% of the aged population, substance use problems affect almost 1% and roughly a quarter of deaths from self-harm are among those aged 60 or above. Substance abuse problems among the aged are frequently missed or misdiagnosed.

Mental health problems are under-identified by healthcare pros and older people themselves, and the stigma surrounding mental illness makes people reluctant to look for assistance.

Multiple social, psychological, and biological factors determine the level of mental health of a person at any point of time. As well as the typical life stressors common to all people, many older adults lose their ability to live independently because of limited mobility, chronic pain, frailty or other mental or physical problems, and require some form of long-term care. In addition, older people are more likely to experience events such as bereavement, a drop in socioeconomic status with retirement, or a disability. All of these factors can result in isolation, loss of independence, loneliness and psychological distress in older people.

Depression can cause great suffering and leads to impaired functioning in daily life. Unipolar depression occurs in 7% of the general elderly population and it accounts for 5.7% of YLDs among over 60 year olds. Depression is both under-diagnosed and undertreated in primary care settings. Symptoms of depression in older adults are often overlooked and untreated because they coincide with other problems encountered by older adults.

It is estimated that 47.5 million people worldwide are living with dementia. The total number of people with dementia is projected to increase to 75.6 million in 2030 and 135.5 million in 2050, with majority of sufferers living in low- and middle-income countries" All were disturbed by WHO's disheartening facts

"Yes, during depression we are mentally and physically feeble. Very well reminds me the past experiences. I was frail and lifeless and my mind failed to solve. I thank dear Azra for rejuvenating me and my psyche. My juvenility is blooming once more. In life things are never the same, sometimes sour and sometimes sweet, you need to taste both to complete the cycle of life. Please heed to the poem I recite now:

Life is spiced,
Sour and sweet,
hot and cold;
At times sad,
At times fun;
Sometimes win,
Sometimes lose;
This is contour,
shade of life;
At times dusk,
At times dawn,
Sometimes good,
Sometimes bad,
Adopt them,
Cling to your heart;
At times dark,
At times bright,
All are mortal,
One to go,
One to come,
All you learn in your life;
This is the shade,
Contour of life;

"In the past, they had contributed to the economic activities, but now demoralized for their grey hair. Yes physically they may be unfit but mentally they may have best to guide. They are the best for social buildup. They can be used in schools, colleges, tutorial, kids care centers and local social activities as they have vast knowledge to deliver. As long as they are active diseases are never nearer to them.

- CBSC and UGC should assign curriculum to the students to study aged and their issues.

- Mingle with them to understand, make reports and submit for eligibility to securing marks.

- Made mandatory for children studying in nursing and biological doctor to visit them and make report for eligibility to appearing final exam.

- Police and Administration training centers too can contribute by making mandatory for achieving final results.

- Purpose of Senior Citizen Act 2007 should also be to engage them in implementation of Act. Seek their physical and mental contribution in police, social work and human right activities.

- Free treatment and medication in all hospitals for senior citizens aged over 80." Paramjeet suggested.

"We have noted down your points. *Travel, meeting the causes physically is the real education that you don't get in books or classrooms*" Darshan said in appreciation.

One person nearly 78, his name was 'Patmanabhan' woefully explained his story "I was a Government employee in Indian Railways. You know the salary those days of an assistant station master. With that meager salary I managed raising children and wife. I spent lavishly on their education so they rise up. One son did B.Tech and the daughter did graduation in Arts."

After a deep sob he continued "I spent money and arranged jewelry and dowry for marrying away my only daughter to suitable husband. Then my son got married and spent my deposit on that too. All my remaining money and some I borrowed for my wife's treatment of cancer. However, my prayer and the endeavor failed when my only partner of my courage, happiness and hope left me to live alone in the world."

Patmanabhan took a deep breath while sobbing and tears were rolling from his eyes, continued saying "The situation changed overtime when my daughter in law bought her own house with the help of her father. My unworthy son showed no courage and I was driven out. Fortunately after my retirement I have pension to mange living, live in rented home. But over time, my loneliness drove me to marry again. There too misfortune did not relinquish me, second wife too died of cancer. Whatever savings I had all got exhausted, all because I did blunder not getting registered for medication after retirement."

Patmanabhan took his handkerchief out of pocket to wipe the tear drops seeping from his dry eyes, said again "I have been knocking my children's doors but abnegated response. I want my kids accept me else I shall have no choice but to commit suicide. Loneliness tortures me, can't live without some body with me. Please tell me what should I do?"

Shankar saddened by his story, said "in our social system after the death of wife or husband, living with another companion is discouraged considering sin.

Especially, widows are disowned by the society are sent to widow homes in religious places. We have to be more open to feel happy for their reunion."

A social study student of master's degree again came up with facts "'As per BBC news magazine report by Rupa Jha, over 4 million women widows struggle to survive with mere as less as rupees 300 per month, resort shelters in religious place settlements in Vrindavan, Banaras and other areas'. The horrific persecution existed since the time of Manu Samhita. Still continue and considered 'sati' as honor in many parts of India. Is still time not yet come to put an end to cruel religious rituals?"

"Where has senior citizens Act gone, what is it doing. Is government's job over after the Act is passed? Follow up they don't care. Is this the democracy where the weak are the victims of strong in this cruel religious society?" Darshan's sounded irritated, malaise clearly reflected in his face.

A social study student of master's degree took out another print out of notation he prepared for his thesis, read out the Statistics on Senior Isolation:

- Loss of a spouse is a major risk factor for loneliness and isolation.
- Physical and emotional isolation often leads to social isolation.
- Feeling of loneliness is extremely hazardous, affects both physical and mental health.
- Ignored seniors by own kin are more likely the victims of humiliation and grave loneliness.
- Weakening physical, mental health contributes to the eeriness, feebleness, memory loss, intellectual decline and risk of dementia.
- Social isolation makes seniors more vulnerable to elder abuse.
- Distancing from seniors increases the risk of mortality.
- Social isolation in seniors is linked to long-term illness, obstinacy, unsocial behavior.
- Loneliness in seniors is a major risk factor for depression, stressfulness and restlessness.
- Loneliness causes high blood pressure and uneven heart beat rate.
- Socially isolated seniors are more pessimistic about the hereafter.
- Isolated seniors are more likely to require long-term care.
- Lonely people are more likely to engage in unhealthy behavior.
- Remaining busy in intellectual activity and volunteering can reduce social isolation and loneliness in seniors. Finally, it serves to block route to negative thinking.
- Loneliness may influence aged into alcoholism, is again bad for already weakening body.
- Past contorted relationship with children, daughter or son in laws too accounts to isolation.

The disturbing facts indicate the cruelty on aging people exist world over. How long the Unending disparagements of ageing people continue?"

"Sex is not the only reason for having a companion. There are more reasons to make them feel like they too are humans" Prem said without any wavering. Neelam watched him opening up his concealed feelings and made up her mind to make him and her widow mother happy living.

Next day a lovely weather, Sun too woke up from exhilarating slumber snooping through a cloudy veil. Love scent strewed to fill enchanting ambiance. Saleem and Azra too were present. All eyes were on newlywed legally husband and married woman. A shout out from the crowd "come... come it's a time, sing a song"

"Ok... ok, no problem," he looked at Azra and said I continue my poem '**Thine eyeful gesture, Touch my heart...**"

Thine eyeful gestures,
Touch my heart;
Transform the ambiance,
Whole world is cute;
Come...come O angel,
Let me fill love,
In thy palliative lap;
Let me gift bliss of space;
Let me fill Ambrosia,
In thy serene soul;
Ye was not,
The world was gloom;
Thou beam of gleam,
Bring luster in life;
Let me fill lyrics of songs,
So ye feel ambiance of spring;
Thou a shore of wavy life,
Thine eyeful gesture,
Touch my heart...

Shankar said "before we start our yoga session I narrate the story of a king" then Waited for some time to recollect from memory, and recited: "Once upon a time a king had organized an exhibition of useful antiques open to civic; choose the best you like, give the reason why you like, and take that home free of cost. Yee... It was free so many flocked from morning to evening to choose one for home. All they took whatever they could. The king watched one little girl wasting time hanging out hither and thither. The king came to her in a last moment of closing the show and said "'O' my sweety, sweet, it's time to close take one what you want"

Sweety sweet held the finger with one hand of the king and then with the other hand pointed to the items she liked "I like this... I like that... and there was no end to her like. Each one she touched she liked"

King said "only one you can pick"

106

Sweety sweet then thought for a while and said "whose exhibition is this?"

The king replied "'O' my sweety sweet my beautiful little girl. I am the king and the exhibition belongs to me"

Sweety sweet then said "you said I can choose only one"

King replied "yes"

Sweety sweet leaped over to hug the king, kissed his cheek "Then I choose you. Why should I choose each one by one and repent for what I don't get?"

Kissing Sweety sweet's cheek, cuddled gently soothing her "why did you choose me when you have so many precious valuable things"

Holding him hard the little sweety sweet said "why should I? When the owner is mine, why should I wander looking hither and thither for what I want? You are mine, so all are mine"

"Ooh! 'So little, so prudent' you little butterfly, I too want you." The king then ordered the chief of the ministers and said "give her all in the exhibition. She deserves this. She has taught, when you accept God, you accept his belongings too"

Resting in king's lap, "I don't need, I have the creator what else I need."

After telling this story Shankar explained "don't wander hither and thither in look for contentment. Be after the creator. When you have the God with you, you have everything."

Iyyer Judge commended the story saying "Finally, it is repletion, we are after"

Shankar stood straight upright and asked to follow the Vrikshasana posture (Tree asana). He raised his right leg folded high up to place on the left thigh. He started guiding stage by stage "Stand straight with arms by the side of your torso, fold your right knee and place the right foot high up on your left thigh. The sole of the foot should be placed flat and firmly near the root of the thigh. Make sure that your left leg is straight. In one case you are comfortably balanced, take a deep breath in, gracefully raise your arms over your head from the side, and bring your palms together in Namaste position. Face straight ahead in your front, at a distant object. A steady gaze helps maintain a steady balance. Ensure that your back stays straight throughout the movement. Your entire physical structure should be taut, like a stretched elastic band. Keep taking in long, deep breaths. With each exhalation, relax the body more and more. Just be with the body and the breath with a gentle smile on your face. With slow exhalation, gently bring down your hands from the sides. You may gently release the right leg. Stand straight as you did at the beginning of the posture. Repeat this pose with the left leg off the ground on the right thigh."

He waited a while and said again "this posture is beneficial for the brain, improves concentration, good for leg, back and arms too."

Shankar maintained silence for some time then said "let us start the social forum"

An aged woman stood up to put forward her destitute state "my name is 'Sarla'. I served a maid in a house of businessman for over 50 years. Besides, after the death of biological mother, I was fully responsible for nurturing a son and his sweet sister. I raised children as true mother and had served the house as own house. Both their kids had married and settle in the same house, I was happily accepted by them. But one day the tragic took a toll when the father of kids demised. I have raised the children since their birth until they were tied off. Later changing situation coerced me to leave the house. With a little piece of money I had managed to make it till today, but now no other origin of income to live on. Is there any law for maids to seek maintenance from the girl and the boy?"

Sarla's agony was not new as she had endured much worst situations all her lifetime. In her childhood, she was a victim of child marriage. The so called husband died the day she arrived at her puberty. Now she was no more than a widow for the society, had no choice but to comply with social order. Fed up of the cruel social restriction she secretly got involved in honey with a middle aged person to escape disconcerting ruthless ambiance. She succeeded, but ended up in a brothel in Delhi.

One day police raided a brothel under immoral traffic prevention Act. She also was among the young ladies brought to the Deputy Commissioner's office. A middle aged business man friend sitting in his room, glanced all one by one, but he stared at the gullible looking girl hiding in shame behind others. He spoke to DCP for her rehabilitation and called her pointing finger towards her "get hither"

Sarla gingerly came close to him and stood trembling, her head bowed down. Worried uncertainty surrounded her, thought in her mind "distress is still chasing me"

"Where have you come from?" The businessman asked

"Chingra" she answered

"Where is it?"

DCP answered "in W Bengal. Of course the poorest in the country"

"How old are you?" The business man asked the girl

"Nineteen"

The businessman paused for a while and looked at DCP to seek his opinion. DCP then asked her to recount her past story. Initially she was quite hesitant but his persuasion coerced her to tell that all happened to her. After hearing all he nodded, saying "giving this cursed girl a chance to live is not bad"

The businessman looked at the girl sympathetic, asked "Do you wish to stay with us?"

She was scared and in hesitation, said "But....."

"Rest we will take care if you wish to escape filthy life" DCP said

Her silent bleak face blossomed in the sweet smile, nodded "yes"

DCP called the Circle inspector and asked him to work arrangement for her release and make sure the brothel house does not chase or harass her. Inspector sought businessman and her signatures in declaration note. She was released and went with the businessman in a huge house. Her major role was to take charge of his ailing wife; she was paid salary for that.

She married a servant, working in the same house which was arranged by the businessman. She lived happily with her husband. But before long she perceived that smile never always lasts in her life, the anathema chased her and husband died of pneumonia. Again life jolted her; she gave birth to a lifeless child. No more tears left in her eyes to seep. Mourn, was her way of life now. Same year unlucky businessman's daughter too died. The additional job to look after the infant of demised daughter, she accepted as her privilege. Her breasts were always ready to feed milk. She nurtured both son and the daughter took charge of all their needs until they were tied. The new arrivals changed the atmosphere. The position today was different non cordial in son's house. She exited the house with whatever sum she got paid.

"Did you ask the maintenance from the son?" Darshan asked

"Yes, twice, but had to hush with words 'Maids are servants not moms'" She answered

"Did you ask the daughter?" the advocate Kaliq asked

"No"

"You should ask? If none of them agree, please revert. We will file petition under the senior citizen's Act. Or other appropriate rules that we will see" Kaliq directed

Saleem's mind floated over the mountains of rhymes "It's my time now to recite poem of two mothers":

You bore seed in womb,
Waited for first glimpse of me,
Gave a chance to live in world,
Gave a chance to embrace
Lush beauty of this world;
The other raises me,
Though she is maid;
Takes me to her lapel,

Live and let live

One breast for me,
One breast for her son,
Adorns advances by me,
Enjoys my first walk,
Adores my first talk;
Fondles me when I weep,
Brolly in thundery rain,
Shade in blazing sun,
She sleeps by my side,
In embroidered bed,
Made by her;
Hugs me gives her warmth,
I am asleep before you come,
I am asleep when you go;
You and she both are moms…
One gave me birth;
one raised to let live in world;

The same day she went to the daughter's house, knocked the door. When opened the door the dame inside could not hold her emotions and started to embrace her. Maid mother then narrated her critical anathema in old age. The optics of both were wet, the dame screamed "why did you not recall me."

"I never wanted to upset you. I imagined you would behave as your brother" she stated

"I saw in you as my mom not the one who gave birth. Biological mom gave birth and passed away. You did more than a mom could have done. How can you have such monstrous thoughts! You are always welcome, above of all, I need you" the dame said

"Will your husband object?" maid mother asked quietly

"Never, he too likes you. This is my commitment" the dame stated

The man came out to see the aged maid mother, said "before jumping to conclusions you should test"

Maid mother's confidence and pathos had lost by continual jolts in her life. However, finally her assumed daughter managed to live her peacefully until she died.

The girls have more attachment than male to their families. That is the reason girls are more jealous, more sensitive for their space in the family. The Women are more caring than the men as the motherhood is concealed inside their instinct. A man builds and a woman adorns that into home. Both have important roles in the foundation of sweet home. When she takes over as mother, things softly shift to paradise. Father becomes the role model and Mother the crown.

After the Yoga session was over Paramjeet and Darshan together went to Gurudwara temple to discuss shelter and food facility to aged people, which was already discussed over the phone with the Granthy.

On the way to the entrance of the temple they saw a blind aged woman lying on the floor begging for alms. Darshan and Paramjeet together went to her, sat close to her, collected all the donated currency and placed at right place.

Darshan asked the aged blind "what made you beg at the religious place?"

"I am now 85 blind and no use for them anymore, so my own children have abandoned me here at God's will" an aged blind whispered in muffled voice.

"Did you not inform anyone?" Paramjeet asked

"Why and for whom? I am in my last days of my life. Even flowers lauded if has juice in it and gives odor. I am dried bloom and no juice in it."

"Can we look for your children?" Darshan asked

"No, they are already burdened, why should they endure the pain because of me? If they were comfortable enough, I am sure they wouldn't have left in roadside to starve like this. I have no grievance, only some number of days have left of my life that too will befall" the aged lady answered.

Paramjeet pulled some money from her purse and tried to handover to the old woman. Darshan held her hand back and said "she doesn't need money"

"Then what?" Paramjeet irritatingly asked

"She needs your shoulder as support" Darshan said

"Yes you are correct. What we need: quarter of food they eat, little bit of respect, a bit of emotional support, a little bit feel of affinity and finally little bit sharing joy and sorrow. We are deprived to even closeness" her blind eyes too seeped achromatic drops. Then she began to recite her story"

"I and my husband were bonded brick workers as a consequence of seeking loan of rupees thousand for our land of thousand square foot. That year rain was not sufficient thus failed yield. The interest and compounded interests together coerced us to repay by giving service. Even we sought children's help to making bricks, worked day and night to feed our eight children and the bastard owner. The owner was so influential that we never dared protest against his ill treatment"

"Does bonded labor still exist?" Paramjeet enquired

"Sporadically, mostly in interior villages" Darshan answered

"Children too are poor doing odd jobs. But... Still, they could still accommodate. The failure to manage my long term ailment may have coerced them to abandon me near the temple" blind aged said and lost in past memory, whispering "all poor endure this stage in old age" Aged woman clarified the cause of abandoning.

Darshan tapped Paramjeet's shoulder and said "let's go inside and pray, will come back with some solution"

They both went inside prayed and then went to the Senior Granthy who was well known to him. Darshan was good welfare contributor so his say never discarded that easily.

"Sat Sree Akaal, come sit" senior Granthy offered seats to both.

Darshan sat on the chair and Paramjeet next to her, said "as together we discussed over the phone we need to organize old age home in Gurudwara complex"

"I have already discussed with the board members. Majority was not in favor as could shift spiritual feelings of some visitors" Granthy shook his head while saying. However, he too was keen in setting up but I am not happy as our purpose is service to the society. So I am going to call another meeting and push forward the responsibility towards society"

Paramjeet humbly requested chief Granthy "there is a blind aged lady. If you can support her by giving shelter. I will fund for her" Paramjeet offered humbly

"No, we don't need money at least for this. It is our duty also. Nevertheless, if you wish you can put in the donation box" Granthy replied

The next moment he thoughtfully said "when we can feed poor and aged then why can't we have shelters for them" a little later again he said "let me check again with the members, will inform you"

Granthy organized the meeting of all the members in next few days and finally reached at a point to set up 50 bed old age home with free ambulance and doctor's facility.

A few days later Darshan and Paramjeet visited again. The aged lady was well rehabilitated; she too showed her keen interest in contributing her service to maintain cleanliness inside temple. Darshan extended his support to construct the old age home.

Paramjeet was so impressed that she could not hold her feelings about Darshan, said "you have sweet nectar inside your heart. I feel it"

Darshan simply smiled and said nothing, but a minute later he pulled her hand and asked to join for a walk.

"When I was alone prior to Saleem, Prem and Stephen. The loneliness had almost killed me, during that period illness had clenched me and I was in the hospital for a month for heart operation.

"When we are busy in the job of whatever kind retains us active we are free from all adversities" Paramjeet consented

"Once children are grown enough to take their own load leave them to their own fate. Don't expect too much from them as they too have their children to take care... this was said by one of my friends

"Yes, you are true. We too did the same way. Leaving mother and father in their own fate. But it wasn't like now. The stressful and fear among children have got over in their way of life." Paramjeet cautiously said

"All aged too need to prepare themselves. Earlier the children were the security now shifted to money and assets. If you them, you have all relationship intact. Children don't love you anymore as were in the history. This is the fact and the grievous story of old age life....."

'Finally what I learnt'

- The isolation lies inside the mind when get hurt emotionally by own blood.

- It's true that fear, irritation, anger evolves as the old age surges, does not mean lost all in the life. Be sweet to caretakers including own kids. Impatience and annoyance only helps helping hand secede.

- Develop penchant and hobby the day you reach puberty, like, book reading, writing, art and crafts, gardening and so on; continue till the last day in bed.

- Learn to 'live the life and live each moment of life',

- Withering face, shriveling body are part of natural continual process, reminds nothing is mortal all to face stages of life as fruit first no taste, then sour, sweet and sour, then the sweet, when sweetness reaches to extreme, rots and falls on ground.

- Find friends and companion of own age to chat and share. Don't hesitate to connect yourself with rest of the world.

- Mental Busy activity gives less scope to loneliness invade the mind.

- Loss of life partner hurts draws pensiveness life. You still have life to live, go get it.

- Children may or may not always have time as they too are mother and father, have responsibilities towards their children. An aged too can contribute

- Think of future when you are in past.

- We exist because of our mother and father. Don't forget benefaction of your creators.

- They are the apparent God and Goddess, you don't find anywhere even not in temple, church and Mosque.

- Taking care of creators (aged mom and pop) is taking care of history.

"I am deserted aged man"

I am deserted aged man,
Searching something,
Fills my lonesome life;
Sitting in chair outside bungalow,
With 4 luxury rooms and 5 maids;
Surrounded by virgin mountains,
All greenery exhilarating view;
fluttering cool dancing lake,
making vibrant teasing sound;
birds sitting on tree too don't spare,
Sing a song " O' lonely lovelorn man,
impish world isn't for you;
It's for couple live in love;
We watch you sit all alone watching us,
We sing and revel in pair;
Cool breeze too attacking me,
Says, you are so cool,
Bring someone who warms you up;
you lonely worth no mountains,
it's a heaven meant for family man;
You can't savor nature's bliss,
unless U'r happy man;
promising thoughts blew my mind,
I have no one share my thoughts,
In this old age,
have no one I can live for;
Not even kids,
they send greetings full of stupid quotes,
And say thank you papa,
you are inspiration of life,
In all occasions receive
junk greeting cards,
Sometimes dump them In waste bin,
I lived for wife and for kids,
Did not remarry was a mistake;
life is Sahara totally dry;
In old age no one wants,
How long carry old age curse;
Many aged suffer,
severe life worst than me;

Live and let live

they dump aged in old age home,
send rubbish greetings,
Happy birthday, father's day,
Happy Christmas happy new year,
sparks pain of already injured;
World is mean live or not,
They don't care;
Greeting cards are no worth,
You stupids don't know,
Aged man only needs,
Someone listen the story I have;
we aged need no much,
but good memories and
a glimpse of kids to live rest of life...